D0888818

FT
11-1

... Not Yet !

Ruminations From A Passenger Ship Captain

Captain Philip Rentell

Philip Rentell

ISBN 0 9512313 1 6

Published by

Blue Water Publications.
Trelewyth. Higher Penair
Truro, Cornwall TR1 1TD
England.

To Richard Trevelyan

First published 1998

© (text) Phillip Rentell. 1998

No part of this publication may be reproduced in any form or by means without the prior written permission of the author.

CONTENTS.

Prologue.

Ruminations from a passenger ship Captain.

In my time as Master on cruise ships I have been asked many questions, and of course some of them repeatedly. To that old favourite, "Have you been at sea all of your life?", I have taken to using the reply that one our guest comedians used when asked if he had lived all his life in Liverpool ..."Not yet!" was the somewhat cutting 'scouse' response, so Greg, thanks for that. To those potential passengers who happen to read this book before coming on my ship, I have worked in the main on ships since I left school in 1969 but I don't intend to retire just yet, providing that the power above us all will allow me to continue until sometime well into the next millennium.

Here lie some of the anecdotes and salty tales that make up almost thirty years of earning ones crust from driving vehicles that float. The answer to many a question may be found within. - "What made you go to sea?". "What does your wife feel about you working on passenger ships?". "Have you ever had any dangerous moments?". "If you're down here talking to us, who's up there driving the ship?".

Quite simply, these are just a few memorable moments taken from a busy career (which I hope is far from over) and takes the reader, who I hope may also turn out to be one of my passengers in the future, from my early days of being wet behind the ears to the end of my first five years in command, by which time I had kept the water from getting into my boots - as well as my ships.

Foreword.

My father was a newsagent/tobacconist in Birmingham, as was his father and grandfather before him. I was brought up in the heart of England and only ever saw the sea when I visited my mothers' parents in Cornwall. In fact the only possible connection I might have had towards a sea-wards bent was my maternal grandfathers' job during the depression - that of being a rivet catcher in the Falmouth ship repair yard.

"So why did you come to sea?" - not quite the most asked question, but nearly.

I went to a very progressive comprehensive school in the mid sixties. Apart from the Duke of Edinburgh award scheme and various other outside pursuits, there was a chance to go cruising with the children from different parts of the country, usually around Easter time and I was fortunate enough when I was just thirteen to spend ten days on the British India ship *Dunera*.

After a voyage from Southampton to Vigo, Lisbon and Cadiz I probably needed little further convincing that this was going to be my career. I could not face following my father into the family business. I hardly saw him as a child because he left home so early and returned so late. I probably saw more of him when I was 'detailed to help' in the shop at weekends and during school holidays.

My first aspirations were to become a Radio Officer. Eventually after three more cruises on the *Nevasa* over the next few years, I settled down to finding out exactly what qualifications I needed (and what I thought I might be capable of achieving) and how my education had to continue once I'd left school. Certainly the local careers office new nothing and even the man from the Shipping Federation tried to put me off.

The rest is really history and my first year is described in the first chapter about the *Worcester*.

This is not meant to be a diary or an autobiography, but really a number of experiences which I started to write down a few years ago. Neither would I like to think that this was the sum total of my professional life to date, in fact there are of course some tales which I cannot tell!

I had no intention of publishing a book, but because I knew so little of my father and family before, I felt it was important that I recorded something for the sake of my child and his children.

I've had to dredge the memory for those anecdotes before I became Master in 1990. Since that time I tended to record the stories, usually after the event but in sufficient time before they became just a hazy blur.

The *Reina Del Mar* was my first passenger ship as a junior officer and so has many happy memories. *Gallic Minch* was really the other side of the coin and it really was one of those ships you suffer for the sake of experience.

An 'interesting' year in Palm Line voyaging to the west coast of North Africa followed before my next recollections, those of Hoverlloyd in 1978. Eight months of racing back and forth across the English Channel at over sixty knots.

I was fortunate enough to spend the next thirteen years in Cunard Line and the three stories of *Queen Elizabeth 2* are just a sample of life during that time. The period when the ship was requisitioned by the Government in 1982 is perhaps the most notable.

'Driving The New Hotel' has been published elsewhere and describes *QE2* after the refit of 1987. 'A week Down Mexico Way' was published in the enthusiasts magazine 'Ships Monthly' and is a down to earth account of a typical cruise from the west coast of America.

Then comes my first five years as Master. In many ways it is indicative of the way our industry has become and for many senior officers who have left the security of British registered ships it will bring back many similar memories. Certainly it was one hell of a steep learning curve! *Scandinavian Saga* was debatably the perfect first command. My relatively short time there was later appreciated when I went to Sembawang Johnson in Singapore where I had to quickly adapt to the 'culture shock' of the Chinese casino player plus sometimes playing the political middleman between ship manager and charterer.

Working as a North Sea pilot was an attempt to have a settled home life with my young family. It also gave me a better understanding of foreign mariners and the stresses they have to undergo by sometimes unscrupulous owners.

My most often recounted tales are the murder which took place upon the *Coral Princess*, the utter shambles on board the *Empress Katerina* and a collision on *The Empress*. Best left for the reader to peruse in due course!

I've ended with another article I had published, 'Ruminations', this time in the Nautical Institute magazine 'Seaways'. Included really because I am so often told that I make it appear so easy to dock a ship, no running around, no panic, etc., etc. Well, most of the time it is like that but for those who think it is easy, this will give a more practical insight. Just don't ask me if you can 'have a go' next time you come on board.

In February 1995 I was fortunate to be in the right place at the right time and was offered the Master's position on board *Carousel*, second ship in the fledgling cruise line of the holiday company Airtours. In the past three years we have gone from strength to strength, satisfying thousands of first time passengers, many of whom are now returning to our ships regularly. Professionally it has been the most rewarding period of my career.

I have deliberately avoided recording my recent stories. (probably to the relief of my Fleet Manager). However, the reader can be assured that as long as there are cruise ships and passengers there will be plenty left to tell - but not for a few years yet.

On board 'Seawing'. December 1997.

The *Worcester.*

In September 1969 I was one of just under a hundred new cadets to join the training ship *Worcester* moored in the Thames off Greenhithe in Kent. We were to be the last full intake for the old ship which had been built in the early 1900's as a training ship, used during the Second World War as a submarine depot ship at Scapa Flow and now finally owned by the Inner London Education Authority. Along with an old Abbey and a swimming pool ashore the establishment was officially named the Merchant Navy College.

I had been for an interview over a year before, but because of my lack of Maths GCE 'O' Level it had been decided I should remain at school to ensure my qualifications. That initial introduction had been an eye opener and my mother was not convinced that I would be suited to the obvious boarding school regimentation that took place in this floating institution.

I can assume that then, like now, when I get something into my mind it becomes a challenge - failure or withdrawal is not something that I easily accept.

The *Worcester* was more than anything character building. In some ways I was fortunate in that I was placed into a small group of young men who were to study for their Ordinary National Diploma, the remainder were taking their Ordinary National Certificate.

From the beginning I found the academic side very difficult and it was quite obvious to me that I would be thrown out after one term. The Physics and

Electronics was another language as I had struggled at school to get a General Science 'O' Level even at the second attempt. Naturally maths was equally as frustrating but some of the other practical subjects such as General Ship Knowledge, Navigation, Seamanship, etc., were more to my liking. I quickly learned to drive boats and enjoyed the outdoor activities on the river even though they were completely new to me.

By the end of the first term the last of the old boys left. They had completed three years and were finally joining whichever shipping company would take them. Even if they had only reached the minimum standard, they had had a good grounding of seamanship and all would make good officers eventually.

I, along with the rest of my small class, was made a Cadet Captain and placed in charge of Mizzen Division. The responsibility, such as it was, took time to sink in. However, the confidence to give orders came quickly but it was not always easy.

I struggled on with my lessons, was not thrown out, and survived the year. Academically I was not brilliant and was eventually placed onto the ONC course for the remainder of my three year cadetship. In fact an OND or an ONC was only useful if you left the sea altogether. The real goal for us was a Second Mates Certificate, the final examination that would allow the cadet to go to sea as a junior officer and take a watch on the bridge.

In the meantime life on the *Worcester* continued and was an experience not easily forgotten. The good times probably did not outweigh the bad, but at the end you knew you had been through the mill, to a proper training ship and not some mamby pamby polytechnic.

The ship had been built out of iron and steel to resemble a larger version of Nelson's *Victory* and, needless to say, was slightly lacking in modern day comforts. When the winter came the chill easterly wind rushed down the Thames across Long Reach, and would come racing through every hole in the ship's side, penetrating the accommodation deck and through anything in it's way - including us. The Orlop Deck was one through space where the deck boards had been rounded by continual polishing and with bunks separated by steel lockers into groups of five or six. Towards the stern was a billiard table wedged up in an attempt to make it horizontal, but it was still affected by the passing river traffic which at times gave the ship a gentle roll.

The Cadet Captains had a private little recreation room to which we could retire away from the other lads and that was next to the hospital where the able, but not so attractive Matron ruled the roost. There were many stories invented about her sexual experiences with previous cadets, but of course there was never a cadet that could give me first hand details of his experiences !

One of the strange characters we had as a lecturer was a certain Mr. Fowler, apparently known as 'Fruity Fowler' to the older boys! Within a few weeks of our arrival he took us to the swimming pool situated in the college grounds ashore in order to demonstrate the function of the inflatable liferaft. The raft was already floating in the pool and after changing he told us to take off our trunks, jump into the water, swim out to the raft and climb in.

We were all very 'green' and, although we thought this a little strange, we obliged and embarrassingly complied with his request. Once inside the raft, the flaps were closed and he, also naked, proceeded to explain that because of the enclosed environment, the raft would soon heat up and thus the cold wet bodies without clothes would soon get over any degree of hypothermia we might have suffered by being in the ocean and remaining in wet clothes.

It was at this moment that another class of senior boys unexpectantly came into the pool area, saw what was happening, started blowing wolf whistles and casting homosexual dispersions. Looking back it was really very funny, but at the time I think we just realised what fools we must have seemed to have been duped like that. Fowler did attempt to assist one of the cadets who, by this time had left the raft, and because he could not swim was shuffling along the wall bar. Needless to say, with so many of us around, nothing untoward happened, but it was my first insight as to what could be considered the 'alternative' society, which could be encountered later on in life.

Our time off was limited to a few hours in the evenings when many of the boys who had a few bob went into the village to the nearest pub. Every other weekend was free after Saturday morning Divisions and so for the first few months, I took the opportunity of visiting a young lady in Rochester who I had met the previous summer. That relationship tailed off and, after a dance we had organised, I used to head the other way and visit another lady in Northfleet. Regrettably she had other plans and went off to be a Bunny Girl in the London's Playboy Club. Pity really because her father was an interesting man, the skipper of the last open wheelhouse London River tug.

We really didn't have much time for protracted affairs, apart from the studies which didn't get any easier as the months progressed. We were obviously also expected to do all sorts of nautical type things. I was in the rowing team for my Division and we had to train by rowing large whalers which were very heavy. There had been a race called the 'Houlders Oars' which used to be pitted against another nautical institution, 'HMS Conway', but they had no team to offer so it was competed in house. Our Division put up a good effort but were placed second.

Undeterred, several of us volunteered to row in a charity race from Gravesend to Southend Pier and back, a distance of twenty five miles. These whalers had fifteen foot ash oars, so the work was back breaking and blister forming. We made the pier by early afternoon, had a short break and struggled back. I should imagine it's probably one of the most physical things I've ever had to do - and I've never felt the urge to repeat the exercise!

Like all boarding schools, there was always one or two of the boys that were brighter, more clumsy, less liked, etc., than others. I was fairly fortunate, apart from being a bit dimmer than the others in my class I was never actively disliked - I don't believe! The Chief Cadet Captain, however, was a bit of a prat. He took his role very seriously and eventually became ostracised by the others, to such a degree that all sorts of tricks were played upon him.

A few of the boys ganged together and started filling all sorts of coupons in papers and very soon there were some very strange articles of womens' underwear along with catalogues, job applications, free samples, etc., landing on board, much to the amusement of all. Eventually the Captain called us all to a meeting and insisted that this tom foolery had to stop otherwise there would be serious trouble!

One early morning we actually carried the Cadet Captain, in his bunk, down one companionway to the deck below which was just above the level of the river. His bunk was placed next to the old submarine access door which was then opened to allow the full force of an easterly gale to blow right over him. He had been asleep until that time and, needless to say, there was much laughter all round when he woke.

In general, life was relatively routine and apart from a few odd bods, all the boys left after one year as young men and went on to a variety of companies. I was fortunate in that I was accepted by British and Commonwealth, a Company which had well over eighty ships at that time, including five large passenger liners on the South African route. I left the college in July 1970 and joined the cargo ship *Clan Malcolm* in Hull docks on 28th of August, the first of a great many vessels I would have, at times, the dubious pleasure to work aboard.

Reina Del Mar

Introduction.

In early 1973 I passed my Second Mates Certificate and was appointed to *Reina Del Mar* as Fourth Officer. I had completed one trip to South Africa as Uncertified Third Officer on the *Clan Ranald* after I had passed 'orals', the results of which were given straight away, but I had to wait until my return for the confirmation of passing the written section of the examination. In those days there was a shortage of officers with a certificate so my Company, British and Commonwealth, were keen to get me away again as soon as possible.

I remember phoning up the office after receiving my results and they asked me what sort of vessel would I like to work upon next? At that time the Union Castle Line, a part of the B and C Group had six major passenger ships and I stated that I felt I had had enough of cargo ships for a while and that could I go on one of the passenger vessels? I was straight away offered the *Windsor Castle* which was one of the regular mail ships running to South Africa and leaving in a few days time. "That was a little to soon" I said, "was there anything else"? When they suggested the *Reina,* as she was affectionately known, I just about fainted. This ship was the cruising vessel and everyones' idea of a dream to work on board. They said I should work for a few weeks as 4th. Officer, second on a watch and thus 'learn the ropes', then I would go up to 3rd. Officer in charge of a watch.

To get such a ship was lucky at the best of times, but just after obtaining my license was amazing. I was still twenty one years old and would have the responsibility of keeping a safe navigational watch on a ship with probably over 1,400 people on board. Twenty years later and in command, I look back and am still surprised at my luck, but it was a great thrill and terrific experience for a young man.

The Cruising Calendar.

Reina Del Mar had been built in 1956 for the Pacific Steam navigation Company (PSNC) to operate on a liner service from the UK to South America. The advent of the jet aeroplane had sealed the fate of that run and, after a few attempts at breaking into the cruise market, she was finally chartered by Union Castle Line. The calendar was basically made up of two week cruises out of Southampton to the Atlantic Isles, Spain, Portugal, North Africa and the Mediterranean during the spring, summer and early autumn. In the winter the ship would leave the UK for South Africa and then operate cruises to South America from Cape Town.

The ship had a reputation as being particularly friendly and there were many passengers who would come back and cruise time after time, including such notable names as Harry Worth the comedian, and Jean Alexander, the actress who played Hilda Ogden in the TV soap *Coronation Street.* The ship had some kind of atmosphere which resulted in a following. Many of the crew had been with the ship for a long time and those that left often came back to visit. It was a very happy ship to work on and consequently there was never a problem in finding new staff or reliefs. My own relief was another young officer who had gone on to do a Nautical Science degree and was more than willing to work during his university vacation time.

Social events.

There was a great deal of socialising on board, along with a considerable amount of drinking, which rarely got out of hand. We all seemed to adapt to working with copious quantities of alcohol in our bodies! The biggest problem was sleep, or the lack of. I started on the 4-8 watch with the Senior

Second Officer as my 'boss'. I had a tiny cabin just behind the bridge, originally designed no doubt for use as a pilots cabin on those rare occurrences when a pilot would 'stay over'. It was behind a heavy steel door which, when opened, just about filled the whole space. After the evening watch it was customary to quickly change, have a few drinks in the 'Coral Lounge', the main passenger lounge which was reputed at that time to have the longest bar afloat, then go down to dinner.

Dinner in the Tourist Class restaurant was always an event, the wine flowed and there was much telling of stories, rude jokes, etc. The British stewards were usually OK but I remember there was one surly grey haired chap who had obviously been around a long time and was not over impressed with us young 'upstarts'. After dinner the group inevitably drifted on to have 'stickies' in another bar and then on to watch whatever entertainment was organised for the passengers. Unlike my later ships in the Cunard Line, entertainment was rather 'home spun'. There was the small band of 'Ronnie Carroll' and his singer wife Celia Nicholls. There was another chap who played the accordion, but in the main the entertainment was performed by the pursers staff. A Cruise Director, Robbie Rutt, had a dedicated few staff who would perform and these were supplemented by other officers when there was a need for a larger chorus or a bigger show. 'Singing Waiters', 'The Can-Can', 'Morris Dancing', etc., were all performed along with other favourites one might expect from the music hall. Needless to say by the time our officers went up on the make shift stage they had consumed vast quantities of booze, to give then confidence, so the mistakes were often far more entertaining than the original show.

After a few weeks on board I moved up to the 8-12 watch, and a bigger cabin on the deck below the bridge, which became my home for the rest of my time on board. There were no toilets or showers in the cabins, consequently it was a short hike down the corridor but no-one minded as we were all great friends - most of the time. The cabins were quite small with a single bunk, sink and a porthole looking forward onto the games deck.

I probably fell in love many times on that ship, but the first was with a girl called Sarah who came on board to operate the disco equipment. She was very outspoken and a real character, but I think a little too much so and consequently only stayed for about six weeks before being fired. By that time however, our relationship had started and she would come down to Southampton every time we returned from a cruise, staying the night in my cabin where I had managed to get another mattress to make a larger bed on the deck. When we sailed for South Africa in November she stood on the quay as we departed. All very emotional!.

Incidents.

In the first few months on board the *Reina* I experienced a few events which were not necessarily of my own making. The first I remember was during a morning watch after we had left the Straights of Gibraltar and were heading west prior to turning towards the north for Lisbon. There had been many other ships but by 1130 hours there was just one relatively close about half a mile on the starboard bow going the same way. I was writing up the deck log book on the folding table at the bridge front when I looked up and immediately became aware that this vessel was at right angles to our track and much closer than before. The ship was making a tight turn to port, crossing our bow ahead of us and then appearing to continue back in towards our port side, I altered course to starboard but the other vessel kept closing. The Master, Captain Reggie Kelso was on inspection so I sounded a short ring on the alarm bells, (which was his signal to come to the bridge straight away) and rang the engine room telegraphs. The other ship had cleared our bow by the time the Captain came racing up the port bridge wing steps. I could see though that unless I went hard to port, the ship would hit us somewhere behind the wheelhouse. Captain Kelso was unable to speak because he was out of breath, but he could see me having the quartermaster turn the wheel towards the other ship. Very quickly our stern skidded out of harms way. At about the same time the other ship went full astern. She cleared us by forty or fifty feet much to my relief and Captain Kelso, after I had explained the sequence of events, praised me for making the right decision. Some fifteen minutes later, when I had retreated to the deck bar for a gin, the Doctor came up and asked what had happened. He had been looking out of the hospital porthole at the time and all he could see was a cargo ship apparently coming straight towards him!

Three other events occurred within about six weeks which made me feel that I might be jinxed. The first I think was when we were undocking in some North African port. The starboard anchor had been used when the vessel docked and I was in charge of the forward mooring deck party. We 'let go' the ropes and started to bring the anchor home. As it cleared the water I gave the signal to the carpenter on the windlass to slow down the capstan and turned to advise the bridge on my radio that the anchor was clear of the water. They did not at first hear so I had to repeat myself. As I did so, the anchor came up into the hawse pipe at great speed and gave a tremendous thump as it was checked by the ship side plating; the carpenter had not slowed down the capstan. I feared the worst and gave instruction for the anchor to be walked out - it would not move.

The next day we tried all sorts of ways to free the jammed stock of the anchor, but it was firmly wedged into the hawse pipe. We had no joy and in fact it was several days later when a welder had to come on board and burn a large hole into the hawse pipe where we believed the anchor stock to be wedged. It worked and the anchor was freed, then the hole was welded back up again, but I felt a fool for letting it happen in the first place.

The second incident was when we left Guadeloupe Island in the Caribbean. A rope had been passed out to a mooring buoy in the stream and it was the intention when we left the berth to heave on the rope to pull the stern clear of the dock. Again I was on stations, but this time down aft. We heaved on the rope and the stern came away nicely. Only when the Captain instructed for the rope to be 'let go' and retrieved from the buoy did we have problems. We slacked off the rope to allow a native craft to come alongside the buoy and let the rope go. It was getting dark but we could see one man jump onto the buoy and attempt to let the rope go but he was having difficulty. The ship started moving ahead so we slacked more rope. I explained the situation to the Captain, this time Alistair Sillars, over the radio. Still no joy, and the ship was still moving ahead. The bosuns' mate had put a turn around the windlass ready to bring the rope back on board, but as fast as he slacked off, the ships' forward momentum kept putting strain on and the man on the buoy eventually jumped back into his boat.

We had paid out a great deal of rope but the Captain still had not slowed down. The rope was beginning to jump dangerously and I shouted for the men to get out of the way before it parted. Captain Sillars gave instruction to just let the rope go over the side but it was too late as one of the sailors had actually made fast another rope to the tail. I watched with surprise as one man came up with his knife and tried to cut the rope, I had visions of the rope parting and the whiplash taking the man over the side. Fortunately another sailor came with an axe. One blow caused the bar tight rope to part - it disappeared over the side. We had lost over one and a half lengths of good mooring line, probably even then worth well over a thousand pounds.

The third event was probably the most expensive. We were docking in Venice and I was again aft. A local tug had come in and taken our towing spring on the port side to assist the ship as we berthed. We were close to being in the position required when secure, and I was supervising a spring and sternline on the starboard side. The Captain called on the radio to see if the port side was clear so that he could go astern on the port engine. I automatically said yes as I knew I had no lines in the water on that side. However, unbeknown to me, the tug had slipped our wire and as the port engine went astern it pulled in the wire which wrapped itself around the port propeller. Too late I realised what had happened as I saw the floating rope tail being drawn into the ships' side and I barely had time to tell the bridge to stop the engine before, with a big bang, the wire snapped at deck level.

Fortunately the ship was to be alongside in Venice for two days as it took all night for the wire to be burned free from its position around the propeller. Yet again I felt an absolute fool but it is these events which, in the end, make you a better officer and an experienced future captain.

Heading South.

The run down to Cape Town was via Madeira, that lovely Portuguese island in the Atlantic. The ship was to take bunkers and leave some mail and after we arrived alongside, the Senior Second Officer and I sat down for a beer before lunch. There developed a problem and the double bottom tank used for holding the fuel was ruptured. At first we were aware only that there would be a delay in sailing so we decided to continue drinking and it was not until much later that we found out that the oil spill in the engine room had resulted in the sealing of the forward machinery space and the shutting down of pumps, etc. This in turn resulted in a sewage back up into the lowest passenger cabins where 'grey water' was coming out of sinks and showers, flooding the carpets.

All the Pursers staff were 'turned to', helping to move belongings and trying to clean the place up. We took a walk down to have a look and quickly took an about turn. We had probably drunk far more than we should have and it wasn't until much later when the ship was just about ready to leave that the Senior Second Officer, George Paxton, remembered about the mail. The next fifteen minutes saw us literally throwing the bags over the boat deck rail onto the dock forty feet below. It was a right shambles and I'm sure there must have been at least a few broken Christmas presents.

South American Cruising.

We made three cruises out of Cape Town with South African and Rhodesian passengers. The average age was probably no more than thirty five to forty so they were a good, young and attractive crowd - it was fun!

Each cruise was thirty days duration, ten days across the South Atlantic, ten days on the coast and ten days back to Cape Town. On each voyage we called first at Rio De Janeiro staying four days, then a day at Santos, three days in Buenos Aires and two days in Montevideo, Uruguay. It was beautiful relaxed cruising and many friends were made with the passengers who were on board for the month. Needless to say there were also many romances, in fact, it was almost impossible for any of the bachelor and sometimes the married officers not to end up between the sheets with one girl or another.

My own affair was on the second voyage when I spied a very attractive lady on the first night. It turned out that she was four years older than I, divorced, and very willing to have a partner for the duration. We spent much of the first ten days together but by the time we reached Brazil I had become bored with her company, which was typical of my somewhat silly attitude in those early years. I tried to let her down gently but she was very upset. In the end, after about five days, the boys felt pity on her and pushed her into my cabin when I was having an afternoon nap. My physical inclinations overcame my mental ones and that was the end of our separation. I seem to remember that by the time we had returned to South Africa I was physically exhausted!

All the ports were very interesting particularly Rio and BA, where I managed to do a little exploring. On our second cruise it was carnival time in Rio. The atmosphere was electric and incredibly noisy most of the time as our ship was docked on the Tourist Wharf right at the bottom of Rio's main street, the Rio Branco. Taped samba music was played constantly and it felt like we were being drugged by the incessant beat. Passengers and crew had a wonderful time ashore but somehow I felt it all a little overwhelming. I did go ashore one evening with friends when the parades were going past, but the streets were so crowded that it seemed you could just get swallowed up in the mass of sweating humanity. I did not feel at all comfortable.

We took a ride on one a bus one evening, making our way down towards the beach area. It was the most amazing bus trip I have ever made with the vehicle careering around corners at break neck speed. It is no wonder that they have a saying in Rio - 'There are only two types of pedestrian in this town, the quick and the dead!'

The atmosphere in all the ports was very Mediterranean. Santos was dirty and a typical sailors town full of squalid bars and poverty. BA had an air of bustling business and Latin efficiency and Montevideo was notable for its' incredibly aged buses and cars, many over fifty years old. I enjoyed them all and so totally different to the ports I had visited before in Africa.

We made friends with a group of South African air force pilots who came on one of the cruises, and after they disembarked, made a fly past of the ship when we left Cape Town where we usually had only one day to re-supply the ship before leaving on the next voyage. I remember though that Alistair Sillars managed to convince the Company we needed an extra day alongside after the second South American trip - to give us all a rest I think the excuse was! Eventually we left for the last time and returned to England for the Spring and a three week cruise to the Caribbean.

Second Season.

After we returned to our Mediterranean schedule I was promoted to Junior Second Officer and given the 12-4 watch. This was a real killer because I was young and didn't want to miss any of the entertainment. I socialised even more and rarely went to bed before the night watch. I can vividly remember staying in the disco until the last possible moment and giving myself just two minutes to race back to my cabin, quickly change and get onto the bridge for midnight. I always felt great at that time because I had downed at least a couple of large gins between 1130 when the Radio Officer, Dave Garbett, had left to go on watch and before I left. Of course, by one in the morning, the combined effects of too much booze and the darkened bridge made me feel very sleepy. It was often a real struggle to keep my eyes open, one I didn't always win.

One particular night I came to the bridge in the same state. I remember sitting down (fatal) between the radars on a sloped plotting table. We always considered that if we dozed off sitting on this table we would fall off the back of it, therefore waking up, albeit with a headache! However, I looked at my watch at one thinking the time was really dragging and then looked at it again and it was two o'clock. I must have been asleep for an hour. I was stunned into awareness, never thinking this would ever happen, but it had and ever since that day I vowed I would never again go onto the bridge having had too much to drink. What had concerned me most was that we were actually only five hours away from the busy Straights of Gibraltar. Another lesson in the learning curve of life, luckily won without mishap.

We went to the West Indies on one voyage, my first time and a total delight. I recall one particular story which I still use now and again at the dinner table. We had an old lady passenger who died one day and, as we had no morgue, she was sewn up in canvas which was weighted at one end. It was traditional for the Bosun's Mate, or whoever did the job, to receive a bottle of whisky and it was also traditional for the last stitch to go through the nose!

Although it had been anticipated to bury the lady at sea that night, we had a message telling us to land her in Antigua, our next port of call. The corpse duly went ashore but just an hour before we were due to sail the next day, she came back - in a coffin. That night arrangements were again made to pass the lady over the stern. The ship was slowed and turned to alleviate some of the wind blowing across the deck.

I came on the bridge at midnight and was shortly afterwards told by the Mate to resume the course and speed. I turned the ship back towards the moonlight and when the Chief Officer arrived on the bridge he remarked that there had been an unusual event. The coffin, upon hitting the water, had broken apart and no-one was sure that the lady was still weighted down in the canvas. We were now heading back towards the spot and I spent the next ten minutes scanning the waves to see if I could see the corpse floating in the moonlight!

Conclusion.

My time on board was accumulating and I realised that soon I would have to go back for my First Mates examination. I became worried that when examined for the orals part I may be at a disadvantage having only worked on a passenger ship since the last time I had presented myself. I therefore asked to be transferred to a cargo ship to broaden my experience. Looking back I also think that I had become physically tired of being on board the *Reina*. I had experienced many things, drunk far too much and somehow had become a different person, one that I didn't really like. The ship had been good for me in many ways but I instinctively knew when it was time to leave. My next ship was to be the bulk carrier *Elbe Ore*. It was to be a very quick return to earth and the realities of 'normal' ships.

Gallic Minch

Introduction.

In mid 1976 I finally managed to pass my First Mates Certificate. It had been somewhat of a struggle mainly due to the introduction of both Electronics and Electricity as two separate subjects out of the six we had to pass to qualify. I have to say that I was pretty useless at both. After I had completed my six months study at the Brunel Polytechnic in Bristol I sat the exam, failed I think the Electronics first, resat a month later and failed the Electricity. I then decided to return to sea with Clan Line and completed a four month trip to India.

On my return I sat the exam again, without really doing any serious study and consequently failed, so I went back to Bristol and studied hard for a month and finally passed at the next attempt. These set backs gave me, a few years later, a greater resolve to study without interruption for Masters. In the meantime, I knew it was time for change and I looked around for a company where I thought I might be promoted to First Mate.

The mid-seventies was a time when there were still a good number of jobs on offer for British Officers. Denholm Maclay were advertising for Mates on mini-bulkers, cargo ships of less than 1,600 tonnes designed to carry cargo in bulk. The contract time was for ten week trips and that appealed so I made enquiries and was invited for an interview in Glasgow.

Denholm Maclay were an offshoot of the Denholm Group a large ship owner and management company. I was offered a Mates job straight away but felt I could better serve if I were to complete a few weeks as Second Mate, thus familiarising myself with the trade.

They appointed me to a twin hatch bulk carrier, the *Gallic Minch.* The intention was that I should complete ten days or so, take a short break then return to another vessel as Mate. The ship was owned by Gallic Shipping, a small independent shipowner in London who had Denholm Maclay manage the vessel which in turn was on long term charter to Jebsens of Norway.

The ship, because of her small size and shallow draught, could go into many ports which larger vessels could not enter. I was to join in Gunness, a village on the River Trent, some considerable distance from the Humber and Hull which the ship would have had to pass to reach its destination. I joined the ship at a small wharf after a tedious journey by rail. The Second Mate was eager to leave but he introduced me to his new wife; the previous voyages had been their 'honeymoon'. When I saw the size of the cabin I was surprised as to how they had managed to live in such cramped conditions and amazed that they were still been speaking to each other!

The voyages were too numerous to mention save to say that it was normal to have two or three discharging ports a week and that we operated from the northern point of Norway down to Poland, Germany, Holland, Belgium, England and northern France. The cargoes were bulk commodities of varying types, coal, iron and other metallic ores; even a white powder, the name of which I forget, but was used in the manufacture of glass.

My initial enthusiasm soon evaporated when we got to sea. Being a small ship she was affected very much by the sea conditions - so was my stomach! Watchkeeping was basically five hours on the bridge followed by five hours off, a very tiring routine as the longest sleep I could hope to get was not more than four and half hours, and then I still had to eat. The food was at best mediocre, but usually quite poor. The Master, a fairly young Chief Officer who had come out of Ben Line, had to fire the first cook. His replacement was 'helped' aboard in Rouen. He stayed for about six weeks during which time I don't think he was ever sober. He had a habit of putting far too much salt into the food during cooking; eventually the Captain told him to leave the salt out altogether, he did but substituted vinegar instead. The food was ghastly and not exactly what you needed on a rough day.

Ten days came and went without any indications of a relief or promotion, and when the captain finally asked what was happening the company told him just to keep me on board for the full ten weeks. I was not impressed.

Collision.

The runs through the fjords of Norway were interesting and it was customary to take a local pilot for the duration of our stay in the inside waters. One voyage I can distinctly remember. We had unloaded our cargo at some remote wharf at the end of yet another fjord and sailed 'light ship' to pass mainly within the sheltered waters to another loading berth some six or eight hours away.

There had been little need to ballast down after discharge because of the short run, consequently the ship was very 'light', the bulbous bow was well out of the water and we were trimmed down by the stern. The aged Norwegian pilot was on the bridge as we approached a small town at the junction of two fjords. We had to turn to starboard to enter a narrow buoyed channel which led under a modern road bridge connecting the town with the land on the opposite side.

The pilot had brought the speed down to about seven knots and we made a steady course into the channel. On the other side of the bridge lay a small port and coming away from one of the jettys we noticed a red hulled cargo ship, even smaller than our own. The ship appeared to be making for the channel to which we were now committed, the pilot believing we could clear the way sooner for her entrance increased speed to Full Ahead on the engine. Our speed must have increased to at least ten knots through the narrow confines of the buoyed channel, however, it became apparent that we could not clear before the other ship arrived, neither did it look as though she was slowing down. In fact the bridge looked deserted, but sailors could be seen battening down the hatchboards.

We could neither slow down or alter course to avoid the impending collision. To turn would have swung our vessel into the parapet of the bridge; to slow down would have just delayed the inevitable. The rapidly unfolding situation gave us mainly a feeling of disbelief. The crew of the other ship realised, too late, what was about to happen and that the point of impact was going to be where they were working. They scattered in every direction as our pilot advised at the last minute to go hard to starboard and full astern on the engine. The stern had just cleared the last buoy on the port quarter, but our actions were to make little difference. The bulbous bow rammed into the starboard side of the other ship with a sickening crunch.

Our momentum appeared checked, but there was just a moment between that first impact and then the continued forward movement of our vessel. The bulb had penetrated the steel shell and then continued for another six to ten feet until we were finally stopped by the main body of our forecastle. The engine, still turning astern, then started to pull us backwards out of the hole we had created and our ship gathered sternway, the bow swung to starboard as the forces acting on the propeller created a turning moment.

For just a few short moments we stood, as though riveted, to the spot.

The other vessel took a distinct list to port and the oval hole, which must have been at least eight feet by four, came out of the water. I can only presume that, fortunately for her, the cargo on board had shifted thus preventing the vessel from sinking rapidly where she lay. In fact she continued to move slowly forward and made for a small jetty on the opposite side of the Fjord. Our pilot turned to the Master and indicated that as the ship appeared to be OK, we may as well proceed on our way! Needless to say that took us completely by surprise and I can remember saying "But that's a hit and run isn't it?"

We put a boat down and the Mate went over to the other vessel which, by that time, had been secured alongside. Details were exchanged and a truck loaded with steel plate and welding gear could be seen coming across the bridge. After a few hours at anchor and no doubt some awkward phone calls by the master to the Company, we continued on our way. Damage to our ship was negligible as the reinforced bulbous bow had taken the full impact.

Strange as it may seem I can remember very little in the way of enquiry after that accident. I had written down the events soon after into a bridge note book and that was taken as evidence. There was a brief interview some two or three weeks later and that was the last I ever heard concerning the incident.

Grounding.

Life continued much as it had before with one port following another, the weather sometimes good, sometimes not so good. A few days in Gdansk, a depressing port in Poland comes to mind, but only because it was a public holiday, the skies and the scenery were grey, cargo work was slow and most of the Poles I saw seemed to be drunk on cheap vodka!

We had another run up the River Trent with a full cargo; the pilot had advised us to wait for the next tide but the Captain insisted we proceed. Unfortunately there was not enough water as the tide receded and we grounded half way up towards Gunness. Much use was made with the engine operating astern and ahead, but to no avail. We were there for the night and at low water we settled onto the mud with about a five degree starboard list and down by the head, a most unusual situation for a ship and very noticeable when lying in your bunk.

The next day the ship came off the mud in her own time and we continued up towards the wharf. As we approached, the intention of the pilot was to drop the starboard anchor and use it to swing the ship through 180 degrees and then dredge the anchor down to the berth, not an uncommon manoeuvre with little ships in constricted waters. Unfortunately he miscalculated and let the anchor go when the ship was still running at about four knots. The ship started to swing but the chain ran out with great momentum with sparks, rust and dried mud flying in every direction. Somewhere near the fourth joining shackle the cable parted, the chain continued over the gypsy and disappeared to the muddy waters below. The ship, by this time, swinging across the river with the engine going full astern, ran gently onto the bank, the pilot being fairly resigned and informing the Captain that it was the only option left if we were to swing the ship around and dock against the tide onto the wharf, which is what eventually occurred. There was no damage to the bow this time either.

Conclusion.

By the time I had completed ten weeks on board the ship I was quite determined that the 'coastal life' was not the one for me. I had come from an established deep sea company looking for quick promotion, instead I received my first introduction into the more industrial and unsympathetic side of our business, where time is money and personal feelings and company loyalty didn't mean a damn. The people on the ship were just there to fill up the numbers and provided you had some sort of license you had the job for as long as you could stand it. I handed in my notice when they asked me to go back to another ship after only two weeks. The office were most surprised, particularly when I also refused promotion to Mate. A few days later, after a couple of phone calls, I went to London, was interviewed by Palm Line and offered a job as Second Officer on board their ship *Ikeja Palm* I was about to be introduced to the joys of the West African trade.

Hoverlloyd.   1978

Introduction.

One of the most interesting jobs I have had was as a Second Officer for Hoverlloyd, a company operating large SRN4 hovercraft between Ramsgate, in Kent and Calais, France. I had first seen one of these ungainly looking machines in 1969 when I was still on my pre-sea training. I was interested even then because of their unusual characteristics, not really a ship and neither a plane.

By 1977 I had a First mates Certificate and was working for Palm Line, running between the UK and Continent to West Africa, interesting ships but hardly romantic destinations. Hoverlloyd advertised in the late autumn for seasonal navigators for the busy periods in 1978. On November 15th., my birthday, I drove down to the International Hoverport for my interview. The day was very windy and the hovercraft service had been cancelled. A good thing perhaps, as it had been the intention of the company to take me over on a familiarisation trip. Knowing what I do now I would almost certainly have been as sick as a dog and that would have been the end of the whole business.

Captain Roger Syms was my 'interrogator' and I was to be his first victim. We started off very well and I even suggested some of the questions he should ask. By 1130 we had had a chat, walked around one of the craft on the pad, had another chat and then retreated to the bar. My birthday was of course used as an excuse and I met a few of the other flight crew, finally leaving around

1430 hours having been offered the job. I was elated knowing it was going to be an interesting time ahead with a good crowd.

Initial Training and Techniques.

In February I went back to do my initial training which was to last approximately a month. The navigator's position in the control cabin was behind the Captain and Flight Engineer. Two basic radars were all that was used, chartwork being neither necessary nor possible with speeds of over sixty knots and considerable vibration. A designated track across the Goodwin Sands and the Channel was maintained where possible by parallel indexing technique using the navigational buoys to keep a horizontal minimum distance of one mile between opposing tracks. With closing speeds of 120 knots plus, the hovercraft on opposing tracks had to ensure this distance was not reduced. Because of the speed and the amount of traffic, it was normal practise to use the six mile range of the radar, not the normal twelve mile as, with that coverage, it was just about impossible to track the increased number of targets.

I had only one crossing with another navigator, then I was on my own. The navigation was not particularly difficult, however, the collision avoidance was a different matter. The Captain had no radar, nor would he have time to use one. He relied totally on the information being fed to him from behind. The company standing rule was not to pass closer than one mile ahead or half a mile astern of a crossing vessel; this caused problems in thick weather when ships tended to follow one another up the channel about a mile apart. The reality was that we would aim for a ship then at the last moment side slip under her stern.

A certain amount of skill had to be developed to get this technique to work well as a hovercraft when turned would continue on it's previous course for quite a distance. God only knows what the other ships thought if they were tracking us on their radar or listening to the growing roar of four Rolls Royce turbines coming at them through the murk!

Information was passed back and forth in the control cabin via radio as the noise caused by the four great propellers was deafening. We wore head phones with boom mikes and it was important to tell the Captain just enough information for him to picture the general situation in his mind without flooding him with useless paraphernalia.

Early Crossings.

Some of my initial crossings in February and March were close to the limits of wind and wave height, force seven and eight feet, in fact by the time we arrived in the middle of the channel they could be considerably over. The craft were most uncomfortable in bad weather and sometimes it was necessary to strap into the specially designed seats. Needless to say the contents of my stomach were shifted in a vertical direction on more than one occasion. The first time I remember was during an early morning flight when I felt the overwhelming 'desire' after about thirty minutes. Even though I tried to fight it, I succumbed, but only for a minute and a bag was always kept handy for such purpose. In these poor weather conditions it was imperative to resume conning as soon as possible. By the time we had arrived in Calais - late of course - I had regained my composure and felt relatively normal. I climbed the ladder to the car deck and walked into one of the passenger compartments, clutching my little bag. The worse for wear passengers had all left, no doubt vowing never to return, and the six stewardess' were all recovering with the aid of a brandy, (this was eight o'clock in the morning!) I made my entrance, held up my bag and asked if anyone would care for cornflakes! Most of the girls feigned disgust and revulsion but the head girl rushed over, took the bag and said, "Oh! You poor thing, would you like a drink?"

During that first month I worked with many of the Captains, enjoying their differing experiences and attitudes, enjoying the work, fine tuning my own abilities and getting a great deal of satisfaction from the responsibility. The final test before qualifying was a return crossing while navigating from behind closed curtains. Going out on March 19th, was fine and the return went well until within about six miles of Ramsgate when I picked up many targets outside the harbour, some crossing our track. The Captain could of course see all the yachts quite easily as it was a fine day with a clear blue sky, but I had to weave my way through them using the radar to advise him, at one stage having to slow down and stop. The ground controller at the hoverport who could see us in the distance, called up to ask if we had a problem. I eventually navigated the craft through to clear water and made the base. The Captain, when commenting on my ability, said I might be a little less than refined, but at least I was safe!

The Season.

Three of us who trained up at that time were passed for working on the craft and our abilities were set to the test over the busy Easter period, after which we were given a month off as our services were not required until the summer schedule started in earnest towards the end of May. By then another ten navigators had passed through the training system and three or four more had failed, I presume because they couldn't mentally adjust to the different style of radar operation and the ability to cope with many targets while doing a high speed.

For about a three month period during the summer the flight crews were designated teams and I was fortunate to have Dennis Ford as my Captain. We all worked well together and I only regret never continuing our friendship or even exchanging Christmas cards. Our average week would consist of three days when three return crossings were made and two days of two crossings. On a three day crossing day the Civil Aviation Authority ruled that we must have a break of two hours after two trips had been completed, consequently those days were quite long, however the two trip days were finished in under five hours.

I used to get quite a kick out of walking across the apron to the craft, climbing up to the control cabin and making ready for sea. Over in Calais the craft would only be on the ground for twenty minutes, forty cars off, forty on and up to two hundred and forty passengers off and on, plus we would take fuel. The crew consisted of three on the flight deck, six stews' and six car deck men whose responsibility it was to lash and unlash the vehicles.

One of the more unusual problems we encountered were the bait diggers who went about their business on the mud in Pegwell Bay, the stretch of coast just to the south of Ramsgate where the hoverport was situated. During low tide there would be a mile or so of 'beach' to cover before reaching open water. The local fishermen would dig anywhere to obtain fresh bait, even within ten feet of the concrete apron. In misty weather they could not be seen until the last moment and quite often continued happily digging with hovercraft roaring past only yards away, feigning complete indifference. There was a well found rumour that one was actually knocked over face down into the mud as a craft turned off the pad and side slipped onto it's departure course. Although no doubt rather upset, the gentleman in question survived unscathed.

On occasion, to obtain our duty free allowance, a few of us would take a crossing during a day off, paying just one pound. After a few hours spent in the supermarket we would return loaded with beer, wine, French cheese, pate and bread. A party that evening inevitably followed. Due to the nature of the trade Hoverlloyd had ensured a plentiful supply of pretty ladies so company was never a problem!

The number of temporary or seasonal employees was usually over a hundred, consequently the company had their own training routine which took a week. I found it very thorough and I have since wished that other shipping companies would practise something similar.

Foggy Crossing.

My training and ability was borne to the test one foggy morning in mid-summer. We left at 0600 hours with zero visibility, the Captain could only just see the concrete twenty five feet below him. All the way over the conditions remained the same. I picked our way through the traffic using the radar and closed Calais Hoverport without any problem from crossing ships. I advised the Captain to reduce speed from sixty knots plus as we came closer and fine tuned the radar until I could make out the shape of the terminal buildings on my scope. We kept reducing speed, the fog remaining thick outside. I picked out the waves gently breaking onto the concrete apron and advised the

Captain that we were no more than twenty feet to the left of the center line. He picked up the three foot wide line visually just about where I said it should be, and still he could not see the buildings! We slowly edged up to the pad and I remember giving a non audible sigh of relief when he could make out the 'spot' and the indistinct shape of the terminal just ten feet ahead. When we went 'off cushion' I felt the need to leave my sticky seat so I made my excuses and wondered around the outside of the craft doing the external checks for the engineer - and taking plenty of deep breaths.

As is often the case with summer fog, by the time we set off on the return journey it had begun to lift, and on arrival at Ramsgate it was yet another sunny day.

'Poleing'

Dennis Ford now and again had me swap seats with our engineer, Ray, to give him some practise navigating and also to let me have a go operating the throttles and 'poleing' - controlling the craft by use of the aircraft style yoke. This controlled the four pylons which held the variable pitch propellers and the four fans which gave the lift air. Along with the foot pedals which operated the two large rudders on the stern, a combination of effects could be made and it was all rather complicated, in much the same way a helicopter differs from a conventional aircraft.

In calm weather it was relatively easy to keep the beast on track, but in anything above wind force three, all the pilots' skill and experience was required. Getting there was only half the battle; avoiding the large holes in the ocean that suddenly appeared in front of you was more important.

The Opposition.

1978 was to see the first flights of the ill fated French Sedam N500. This much larger hovercraft was to enter service for SNCF, the French Railways connection with Seaspeed, the British Rail opposition based in Dover. Unfortunately the first of a pair had been burned out the previous year during building and the remaining craft, *Ingenieur Jean Bertin*, proved to be very

37

unwieldy. They had major problems with skirt design and reliability which eventually caused the machine to be scrapped. As far as we were concerned, we endeavoured to keep well away when it was manoeuvring as it rarely seemed to make the position allocated on the apron.

The stretched *Super 4* introduced by Seaspeed from Dover the same year seemed to be a far better option and it was considered Hoverlloyd might convert their craft in a similar manner to take advantage of the increase in trade. This was not to be however, and in late 1981 Hoverlloyd amalgamated with Seaspeed to form Hoverspeed and the terminal in Pegwell Bay was closed down. A great pity as it was obviously far better suited than the constricted new terminal built within the Western Docks at Dover.

The Last Day.

The season tailed off by September and it was a case of first in, first out. I had already been interviewed by Cunard Line and was to join the *Queen Elizabeth 2* on September 18th. September 10th was to be my last day on the craft. We made one return crossing around lunchtime, had a two hour break, then left again at 1632 hours. The weather had taken a turn for the worse and there was a blow in the channel, but not sufficient to be above normal craft limits. About ten minutes before arrival in Calais we received a radio message from the port asking us to keep an eye open for a French yacht in distress.

We saw him shortly afterwards and the craft commander, Captain Childs, attempted to close towards the boat, the sails of which were flapping madly in the wind. I made my way to the center passenger door and with the car deck men behind, opened up and prepared to throw a line. From the elevated height of about fifteen feet above the sea I envisaged problems and had no real idea how to overcome them. On the first pass the skipper of the yacht appeared dazed and there was blood running down his face. He caught the line but was to slow in making it secure. The yacht continued into the murk.

We circled the hovercraft and on the second attempt came down off cushion. The yacht approached again and as it passed I jumped down into it's cockpit, quickly taking a turn with the line on the nearest cleat, thus preventing my impending departure in a boat for which I was not in the least capable of navigating. I rushed forward and dropped the jib then what remained of the main sail - it looked as though the boom had swung wildly and hit the skipper on the head, thus causing his apparent inability. A frightened looking woman emerged from the little cabin with a child in her arms. I manhandled them both up to the waiting arms of the car deck crew and then shoved the man in the same direction.

By this time a large workboat had come out from Calais and landed clumsily alongside the hovercraft, rupturing the plenum chamber in the process, unbeknown to us at the time. They took the yacht in tow and I returned dripping wet to the control cabin, passing our wide eyed passengers on the way. Captain Childs attempted to resume passage but the external damage prevented the craft rising onto cushion, the fans being unable to push the water out from underneath. There was no danger of the craft sinking as the inherent buoyancy from many sealed duralamin compartments guaranteed floatation. We eventually 'boated' into the hoverport, gushing great quantities of spray as we crossed onto the apron.

The casualties went ashore along with the passengers and an external examination revealed two holes in the side of the craft. The damage would have to have a temporary repair before a return crossing could be made, consequently the whole crew had to return as passengers on the next available flight. Some sight I must have looked and an unusual end to a particularly interesting season. After 446 crossings of the English Channel in 1978 my official log book finally ended in France.

Queen Elizabeth 2

Introduction.

I joined the Cunard Line on September 18th 1978. After working for Hoverlloyd for over seven months as a seasonal Second Officer I had applied to both P & O and Cunard on the off chance they might have vacancies on their passenger vessels. My enthusiasm for cargo ships had waned and I felt that if I had to go to sea I might as well do so in relative comfort.

The *Queen Elizabeth 2* looked very large as I walked down the Ocean Terminal in Southampton at seven in the morning. I had been advised by the office to be early, but they never told the ship, consequently only the night security watch were around when I boarded. Soon my presence was announced and Roland Hasell, the Chief Officer, showed me the Mates Office and promptly gave me some paper work to read.

I was soon to meet the other deck officers and then my introduction to the ship commenced. It truly is a huge ship to find your way around and takes months, not weeks or days, before you can feel fairly familiar with all the nooks and crannies one finds on a passenger ship.

My watch was to be the 12-4 (hardly surprising) and the senior watchkeeper was an Australian First Officer, John Farroll, rather fat and a little too self assured. Now here was a man with some kind of problem. He always seemed to bring the conversation back to what he had done and how good he was. He had been in Vietnam carrying ammunition on an Australian ship when it had been attacked and he was invalided out with some sort of shrapnel wound to his behind. The Engineers on my watch asked me how I found this rather pompous Mate? My reply caused some amusement, "He's the only guy I know who's had his arse shot off but still talks out of it!"

Although the ship often travelled at 28 knots, I found that it was not particularly difficult to navigate, but being a lowly Second Officer I was really a glorified 'gofer'; I put positions on the chart, logged the in and out telexes, answered the phone, etc. The most important responsibility I was given was looking after the uniform locker, a tedious task made worse by the fact the previous incumbent had totally cocked up the inventory. After the responsibility of navigating a hovercraft it was all a bit of a come down.

One of my first unusual experiences was after a week or so on board, I went onto the bridge just before midnight to hear a big row going on in the 'barn', the space behind the bridge where the quartermaster and bridge boy sat when not required for look out duty. John Farroll went to see what was happening and found himself accosted by a drunken and half crazed QM who was throwing furniture around. The QM shot off down below and Farroll followed him leaving me to navigate on my own. Some five minutes later I heard over the walkie talkie that the QM had barricaded himself into his cabin with the Chief Officer who he was holding at knife point!

This was, needless to say, not what I expected of Cunard Line staff, but anyway I was quite happy out of harms way while the others were being heroes down below. A short while later, Alan Bennell, the Staff Captain, came to the bridge, no doubt to see whether I could handle the navigating 'on my own'. He was quite a character (dying of cancer some ten years later) and instructed me to go and get him a gin and tonic. I thought perhaps this was a little unusual, on the bridge of the *QE2* in the middle of the night, anyway I was prepared to play along and asked him if he wanted ice and lemon. Of course he did and was most upset when I said he had no ice left in his cabin - he sent me off to find some with the remark, "Come on Rentell, how do you expect me to drink gin with no ice?" He soon realised that driving the *QE2* on my own was not beyond my capability and soon left me to my own devices. Farroll appeared another hour or so later after they had managed to sedate the sailor and lock him up.

There were over the period of ten years working on board *QE2* many incidents of one sort or another - fires, grounding, bad weather, deaths - but I don't remember a birth.

Bad weather

I was on the 8-12 watch with Dan Robinson and we were approaching New York on a dark and very rainy night. The Nantucket light vessel was some miles behind us and the ship was steaming at close to 29 knots on a course of 270 degrees, due west. The radars were completely blocked out by the intensity of the rain but the visibility still appeared to be reasonable.

I was behind the chart table poring over some magazine or paperwork and Dan was keeping the visual watch with the quartermaster. He called to me saying that he thought he would have to alter course for a crossing ship; this was fairly unusual on this stretch so I asked him to hold on while I tried to pick the other vessel up on radar. The screen was completely blotted out and no adjustment of the rain clutter control made any difference. I could see the faint red light of the ship fine on our starboard bow so I told Dan to alter the course on the auto pilot.

We had a new adaptive auto pilot under trial and Dan turned the dial, the ship began to change course, but then seemed to slow down and the other vessel was getting close very quickly. The adaptive auto pilot had the rate of turn set into it, and it wasn't fast enough! The visibility was obviously a lot less than we thought and the oncoming ship must have been a lot closer than we first believed. Just at that moment, the Staff Captain phoned up and started to waffle on about a morning call, I was getting impatient to get over and change auto pilots and had to hurry him off the line.

I put the helm hard to starboard and the ship started to race around taking a list to port, but the oncoming vessel still seemed to stay on the same bearing fine to starboard. Quickly the red light became several small lights and it was possible to see the shape of the other vessel, which was a cargo ship of about 3000 gross tonnes. In a mere moment of time the hull of the other ship disappeared below our bow and, as we continued to turn, the masts and bridge of the ship raced past onto the port side, missing us by no more than twenty feet or so.

The final moments passed so quickly that it was almost a blur on our conscious, but it had happened and after I put the helm over the other way, I was just in time to see the other ship disappear into the darkness. We were incredibly lucky not to have had a collision and I can only presume that the watch on the other ship had not been very attentive as they never attempted to alter course.

The end of the watch was only twenty minutes away and I told Dan to leave any talking to me, I didn't really want some major enquiry going on if I could help it. Unfortunately quite a few people in the night club had seen the lights race past the window and we were barraged with questions. I told Captain Arnott next morning, but he showed little interest, no doubt he'd been through similar experiences in his long career and knew that they happen now and again. He was that sort of chap, never ruffled, never got excited, never raised his voice - well respected by us all.

There were of course many occasions when the ship had bad weather, common on the Atlantic in the autumn and winter. Freezing cold conditions were often experienced in New York around the Christmas period when, on occasion, the Hudson would freeze around the ship. Those early mornings on the forecastle were a bitter experience, wrapped up to the nines but the cold permeating every layer of clothing. I had to lay the anchor out one night when we went on a cruise to nowhere. Captain Ridley decided he wanted to use the spot we had used a few nights before and I was on the fore deck for over an hour in very strong wind conditions when the chill factor brought the temperature down to something like minus twenty. We tried to get whatever shelter we could behind the windless machinery and when I actually had to stand out on the platform overhanging the bow, the wind actually went straight up my trouser leg! An anchor has never been laid out so quickly before and Ridley, obviously feeling at least some pity, invited me up for a shot afterwards. I could not hold the glass as my hands, slowly thawing, were very painful.

Grounding.

The first time I remember going aground was leaving Port Everglades at the start of the 1979 World Cruise; there was a strong wind coming up from the south and as we crept through the channel I felt the ship lurch to starboard twice. The Bosun's Mate aft, where I was on stations, thought it had been a tug, however, we had actually bounced off the bank of the dredged channel on the port side. Captain Portet had of course kept his implacable cool and just increased speed to ensure we didn't become stuck. In fact the damage was restricted to the port bilge keel which had torn from the hull over thirty or forty feet. A weld had cracked and one fuel tank became contaminated with sea water. The damage was eventually repaired at the next refit.

The second occasion was far more serious. Captain Jackson was in command as we approached San Juan, Puerto Rico, and there was again a strong wind blowing onto the beam. San Juan is not an easy approach as there is an almost ninety degree turn not long after the entrance and it is necessary to keep speed on to make the turn and counteract the drift effect of the wind. Unfortunately we probably had too much speed and we side swiped the starboard hand buoy, eventually coming to stop resting on the right hand side of the channel with the buoy dangerously close to the propellers.

All the tugs came out to assist, but the ship was well stuck and the Captain did not want to use the starboard engine in case of dragging the buoy and its chain into the prop. After some four or five hours a large dredger working in the harbour came and manoeuvred off our stern and took two of our steel mooring wires. The combined effort plus a last ditch effort with both propellers pulled the ship off, breaking one of the wires at the same time.

We were pulled to the berth, towing the buoy and its chain in at the same time. Divers were sent down and we found that the buoy chain had actually become trapped, not around the propeller, but above the rudder close to the stock. The divers worked all night to release it and in fact had to take turns,

44

sawing through the heavy chain with a hacksaw. Fortunately there was little other damage except to the underwater hull paintwork.

Only a few weeks later we went aground again, going into Barbados. I had set up the ship for the approach and handed over to Peter Jackson explaining that I had about five degrees on to counteract the northerly set. The young pilot came onto the bridge, saw that we were apparently heading for the breakwater and instructed the quarter master to go hard a port. He then realised his mistake and put opposite helm on, but it was to late. The ship set up to the left and in fact to miss the port hand buoy he tried to bring the bow to port again. Of course, the Captain could see we were fast running out of water in front and instructed the engines to be put astern. We lost steerage and landed gently onto the side of the channel, again with our stern perilously close to the buoy.

The ship remained stationary for an hour or so, rolling gently with the swell, but touching the bottom as she rolled to port. Captain Jackson eventually took the bit between the teeth, went full astern on both engines and we gradually pulled off the bank, this time without the buoy.

After gaining sufficient space we made a new approach and docked without further incident, again there was no damage except to the paintwork. For sure the QE2 was a strongly built ship, designed for the pounding from the north Atlantic and thus able to accept these minor excursions onto 'the putty'.

Fires.

Within twelve months of my being on board we had the most serious fire that I experienced on the ship. In the middle of the night a crew member had gone into the galley of the "Tables of the World" restaurant, normally closed down at night, and had used one of the ranges to cook a meal. The range had been left on with a pan of fat left sitting on top. The fat eventually self ignited and filled the galley with smoke.

The alarm was raised and two fire teams mustered, they entered the galley from forward and aft, but the smoke was so thick that it took them twenty minutes to find the source of the fire. Fortunately the flames had not taken hold inside the vent trunking and they were extinguished relatively quickly with hoses and CO_2 gas. We learned that there was a great deal of enthusiasm to use the fire equipment; at one stage there must have been at least twelve sets of breathing apparatus in use, which probably is not a very co-ordinated use of resources because we couldn't recharge air bottles as fast as they were being used.

The galley was a mess, the smoke damage was quite incredible with all surfaces black and greasy. The staff made a superb effort and by the morning, breakfast was again being served.

Another fire was rather unusual as it was in a vacuum cleaner bag. The cleaner had most probably sucked up a still burning cigarette and then been left on a crew stairwell. Late into the night a report of smoke was received from the crew galley two decks above and the sailors night gang went into action. There was a tremendous amount of smoke, completely filling the stairwell which covered about five decks. The smoke was seeping through the edges of fire doors on different levels and being recirculated around the air conditioning system. When the cleaner was found it was soon extinguished and we presumed that the cigarette had slowly caused the debris in the bag to self ignite.

Suicide.

We had one slightly bizarre suicide while I was on board, a male passenger who was travelling alone in a penthouse cabin during a ten day Caribbean cruise from New York. The steward called our attention to the cabin which had not been slept in and in which the tipping envelopes for the different staff had been carefully placed on the desk. Upon investigation it would appear that the gentleman, who was only in his thirties, had dined mostly in his cabin, had befriended just one other couple who had also dined with him on occasion.

He had for some obscure reason taken apart the lifejacket from the closet, removed the floatation polystyrene and stuffed the blocks into a drawer along with the cords for securing the lifejacket. The orange exterior material was missing. Also missing was one of the towelling robes placed in the cabin along with the cord from the spare one - he had always insisted that the steward provide two clean robes each day.

There was little we could do, it appeared that he had climbed out over his balcony some time during the night, climbed across the lifeboat which was opposite and then just jumped into the water - a distance of at least sixty feet. After several hours of searching the ship, the Captain decided that it would be fruitless to turn the vessel around and a report was therefore made to the authorities. A mystery of the sea.

Captains.

The first Captain I sailed with on *QE2* was Captain Lawrence Portet. He was a very tall man, over six feet four and perhaps the most eccentric. His manner was rather rigid and he could not be considered a great conversationalist. I was just a junior and therefore rated well down the scale when it came to social intercourse, even orders usually came through the senior watchkeeper. I was to know him a little better after he returned to the ship in the mid eighties.

Captain Douglas Ridley was the Staff Captain who first did relieving voyages as Master, a formidable man with an amazing IQ and memory who it was very unwise to cross or suggest that he may be incorrect. If an officer tried to hide a mistake he would soon know about it and a furious tirade would descend upon the unfortunate. He later became General Manager and Commodore and I became trusted by him, not because I was always right, but because I was fairly quick with the sums when he wanted an answer and because I was honest enough to tell him when I'd cocked up.

He sent me out to South America to investigate the ports of Valparaiso in Chile and Callao (Lima) in Peru, to ascertain whether the ship could berth and also whether they could supply the fresh water, fuel, stores, etc., that she might need to accomplish a round South America voyage. That was my first introduction into the world of ship management and planning and I found it absolutely fascinating, I even took the initiative of flying down to Puerto Monte, an anchor port in the middle of Chile close to volcanoes and lakes. I felt great satisfaction when the ship made the voyage some two years later.

One particular story remains in my memory. I was navigator of the ship and Ridley phoned me up one evening to check the distance to the next island in the Caribbean. I quickly checked the course card and informed him He made the decision there and then to sail later. After checking again I realised I had made a mistake and had told him the course instead of the distance; fortunately it was not going to be a problem, but even so, I knew he would check himself later and find out. The other guys on the bridge visibly winced when I told them my mistake. There was no way out, I had to go and tell him.

I found him in the Chief Officer's cabin with about ten other senior officers having a drink. I knocked, apologised for entering and told him my error. The other officers in the room went silent, Ridley's face was a picture, one of severity but also I could see he was playing with numbers in his head. He asked me what time was sunrise the next day, obviously with a view to arriving at first light. This time I did not readily know so I phoned the bridge from the cabin and asked John Scott, one of the Second Officers, to check our prepared sunrise table. Being Australian and somewhat of a character, he immediately said, "What's the matter, are you going to be shot at dawn?" This was quite audible to the other officers in the room and they had a hell of a job to control their laughter; meanwhile Ridley looked like thunder and I, red with embarrassment, just asked Scott to read the 'bloody table!'

Captain Peter Jackson came next, a short man who was an accomplished pianist. I liked him very much, not because he was just a total contrast to Lawrence, but because he was very approachable and always seemed very humble. He trusted his officers, allowed them to 'have the ship' sooner and for longer, thus giving them more job satisfaction. Somehow I had the impression that, even though he was obviously a very experienced seaman, he held the *QE2* in some sort of awe. Peter was the Captain who took the ship down to the South Atlantic during the 1982 Falklands crisis. Regrettably I think he made his feelings known about the management style of the office in

New York and they in turn allowed him to retire from the ship with little ceremony when his time came, unusual for a Captain of the *QE2*.

Next came Captain Robert Arnott, a tall, well built man who lived near Blackpool. He was an incredibly popular Captain, respected by passengers and crew alike. Never visibly became angry, unflappable and obviously a great socialite who could keep people amused with his stories. He had a lovely north west accent which belied his position as Master of the world's most prestigious liner. He eventually retired in the mid eighties and the Company helicopter was flown onto the after deck to lift him off, a big public relations ploy, with his officers lined up to wish him well. In fact the helicopter took him to the local airport in Southampton and Captain Bob came back by taxi to pick up his bags.

Lawrence Portet then followed and stayed until the major refit in 1987; he was at times one of the most pedantic of Masters. I don't think he really got on very well with anyone, but as a result of his unusual manner I have several after dinner type stories which usually cause a laugh or two.

Because of his height he always looked down at me and his voice was at times very condescending. He allowed me up on more than one occasion because I didn't do exactly what he asked or because I tried to suggest a different way; in the end I think he grudgingly respected my ability. By the time he was due to retire I had known him for almost ten years, on and off. I offered him my best wishes, he looked at me and said, after considerable thought, "Thank you Rentell for your good works over the years, it's been .... interesting!"

One his most memorable comments was apparently made during a World Cruise with the ship heading through the bay towards Yokohama. The little Japanese pilot was rushing from one side of the bridge to another panicking because of the number of fishing boats which were blocking the way. Lawrence eventually had had enough of this and went off to the bridge wing and took to walking up and down outside, seemingly oblivious to whatever was happening elsewhere. The Chief Officer came out and mentioned that the pilot was a bit of a worrier to which Lawrence replied, pointing first to the medals on his blues uniform and then in towards the wheelhouse - " I got these for killing those" - and continued walking.

Allan Bennell followed on from Lawrence and took command not long after the ship had had the major refit when the steam turbines had been removed and a diesel electric plant had been installed. He was another interesting character, quite a ladies man, and a sad loss when he died with cancer just a year or so later.

I remember one occasion when the ship was alongside in Southampton during the night of the big storm of '87. The wind was well in excess of fifty knots blowing onto the starboard quarter and fortunately pushing the ship onto the dock. I came up to the bridge in the early hours, unable to sleep because of the noise. Alan and I spent most of the night up there waiting for the wind to veer and possibly push the ship off the dock as it went round to the port quarter. There would have been little we could have done except release the wire mooring lines before they broke and drop the anchor, and just hope it would not drag allowing the ship to go aground onto the bank on the other side of the river. No tugs were available as they were attending a supertanker which had broken from it's moorings down at Fawley.

Fortunately the wind began to moderate without veering during the early daylight hours, we remained safe alongside, but a dockside crane had blown over and throughout southern England there was considerable damage to trees and buildings.

Alan's relief was Robin Woodall who was to take over and stay until 1994 when he finally retired from the ship. Another very tall man, Robin was well liked and a totally different kettle of fish from Lawrence, very approachable, experienced and happy to delegate in order to educate his subordinates.

Trivia.

Amongst others, we had two rather famous names that I managed to meet, Larry Hagman, the famous J.R. from the TV series *Dallas* and Loretta Swit, better known as Hot Lips Hoolahan from the film *Mash*. I met them both at the Officers Wardroom cocktail party which was a regular event each voyage. Larry Hagman I arranged to show the bridge the next day after which I took him down for a drink afterwards - he managed to get through many shots of Bacardi before leaving for lunch. Loretta Swit came up to the bridge with her chaperone, a man of much younger years. She did not appear so impressed but did ask if she could use the 'Ladies Room'. She was pointed in the direction of the not so salubrious bridge toilet and came out after a few minutes or so. Being the type of chap I am, I asked if she would mind if we had a small plaque made and put up in the loo - 'Hot Lips Sat Here'. Funnily enough she did not seem very amused!

There was at times a very good atmosphere on the ship, particularly on world cruises. I used to organise, once a year, a special train party, the theme of which I'd learned from someone else some time before. The basic plan was that the party was based on a train timetable with different cabins being stations. At each station the train would stop for twenty minutes and a different cocktail was served. There would be five minutes travelling time between each station and where ever possible passenger alleyways were not to be used. There was a driver, conductor and a guard and the timetable had to be rigidly adhered to. There would be no more than eight or nine stations and no more than twenty or so staff, definitely no passengers. Needless to say that by the end of a train party there would be some very inebriated people as it was almost a challenge to make the most outlandish cocktail. One of mine was 'After Eight Mints' - a concoction of Creme De Menthe, Kahlua, with whipped cream on the top! Quite foul really, especially if it's the ninth different one you've had. On that particular occasion the cream bowl ended up on my head and cream was flicked all round the room - what a smell the next day and one that lasted for weeks, even after constant cleaning!

I was not so stupid as to go to the full party as I inevitably organised it when I was on the 8 to 12 watch and therefore joined in half way through after midnight. I heard on one occasion when Captain Jackson was in command, that he had heard of the event and was somewhat disappointed he was not invited. I quickly put him on the guest list and sent an invitation. He went to the first station, which apparently was a little slow to get going and consequently caused a diversion to his quarters. I later saw him just before midnight and he explained he had decided it was time to leave the party when he came across the 12 - 4 Second Officer playing the piano in the main deck Rotunda with a great palm leaf sticking out of his ear!

Queen Elizabeth 2

THE FALKLANDS.

In 1982 the Argentine Government landed troops on the British Dependencies of South Georgia and the Falkland Islands, taking control of those remote South Atlantic Islands by force. The British Government, in response, told the Argentines to leave or they would in turn send troops to recapture the territory. The Argentines did not voluntarily leave so a task force was rapidly assembled and proceeded south.

Requisitioned.

After the P&O liner *Canberra* had been requisitioned, it occurred to me one night on the bridge, that *QE2* would be a logical next step in the moving of a large number of back up troops to the Falklands. I didn't particularly relish the thought of giving up our pleasant summer cruising schedule, in particular our Northern Capitals cruise in July when I had planned an event in the Geiranger Fjord with a Norwegian hot air balloon enthusiast who had come down to the ship on previous calls and launched his balloon, complete with me in the basket on two occasions, from the back end of the ship. This year we were to attempt something new which involved a hired float plane plus me and my skydiving sports parachute!

Going into the southern winter didn't appeal either. Being at sea for seven months of the year makes the average 'jolly jack' appreciate our brief glimpses of the British seasons, particularly the spring, which if I miss, I always feel cheated. However, I still had that childish irresponsible sense of adventure and this appeared to be right up my street.

Second Officer Paul Jowett and myself were responsible for the 8 to 12 bridge watch. The trip had been interesting with a first time call at Philadelphia where we had stayed for three days to start off their festivities for the founding of the city two hundred years ago. During our time in the port, over 12,000 guests had come aboard to tour the ship. The carefully organised program had allowed for 500 coming for breakfast, 1,500 for lunch, 1,000 for afternoon cocktails and 2,000 for a dinner dance each evening.

One would be correct in thinking that we would be glad to return to the normality of driving the ship which is, I suppose, much like piloting an aircraft, once we get the 'meaty bits' of navigation out of the way, one appears to be doing nothing except looking out of the window. Actually it's called 'execution and monitoring' by the Department of Transport. The result though is that, at times, I get the desire to get the brain to tick over a little faster by finding work for it to chew on. I decided to do the sums necessary to get the ship to the Falklands - approximately 8,000 miles by direct route from Southampton, ten and a half days steaming at 27.5 knots, our economical top speed. The ship has been known to do 30 knots at times, but this would depend on displacement (weight), weather and another factor not often realised by the layman, the sea temperature. The warmer the sea temperature, the harder it is to condense the recirculated distilled water, which is used to make steam to power the turbines - and we would of course have to cross the equator. We could just about make it on 'one tank', but we wouldn't have very much fuel left when we arrived. We would use just under 6,000 tonnes, which at $180 per tonne, would cost over a million dollars.

These scraps of useless information I passed onto Captain Alex Hutcheson, the relieving Captain of *QE2*, when he came up to the bridge after dinner one evening. His only comment was,

"You two will have us down there.....!"

I believe he thought it most unlikely that such an event would take place, however he was I think pleased to have the information at hand a few days later when being quizzed by a radio reporter.

On Monday 3rd May I was invited to one of the Penthouse passenger Suites for a lunchtime drink and it was on the way up that one of the nurses, on passing a group of us, passed the news that the BBC had just announced that the ship was to be requisitioned as a troop ship. We stood there almost in a state of shock. Naturally we did the only thing you can do in that situation, have a drink! The conversation though was a little stilted and nervous. Little did I realise then that the very room in which we were drinking champagne would be the one General Moore, the designated Commander of the Falkland land forces, would be moving into when we reached Ascension Island.

I had to go back to the bridge just before 1300 Hours and found out that the report was true and that Captain Hutcheson had been phoned up by the BBC and asked whether he was aware of the decision. He could only answer "No!". It is a great pity that Cunard Line could not have phoned the Captain first. After that we could only listen to the radio broadcasts which were now easily received as we were rapidly closing the south coast and due to arrive in Southampton that evening. The atmosphere around the whole ship was one of being gently stunned.

The take over.

In the morning of the following day I went up to the bridge before eight to find a Royal Navy Lieutenant Commander, in civilian clothes, poring over numerous plans of the ship, scrawling jottings down on paper and saying this was the third ship he had been given to put helicopter pads on. I walked around the open decks with him and the Chief Officer, Ron Warwick, and was slightly amazed to hear him say,

"Oh yes, I think we can chop this lot off here" and "fill the pool full of cement to take the load off the flight deck supports".

Certainly it was something I had never envisaged happening to any ship I worked on, yet alone the *Queen Elizabeth 2* on which I had now served for over three and a half years and felt was a part of my life.

For sometime during that day, while endless meetings were taking place, we knew nothing of what was going to happen to each of us. I was due to go on leave for three weeks however I suggested to the Staff Captain that I was willing to change places if any of the other married bridge officers wanted to stay at home.

Captain Douglas Ridley, then serving as Executive Captain on board (a slightly grandiose title for General Manager), tracked me down after yet another hydraulic lunch and asked me which courses I had done in the Royal Naval Reserve. Only one in fact, the Introductory course at Dartmouth a few months before, and I had only joined in a bout of enthusiasm some six months previously. Ridley wanted me to sail with the ship as Liaison Officer, acting for both Cunard Line and assisting the Royal Navy party which we would be carrying. I was later introduced to Captain 'Jimmy' James who would be my new boss. He said he would like me in RNR uniform and I was therefore allowed to plead for a few days home leave to go and collect my gear.

I went home by train with a sort of satisfied feeling, believing that I was going to be involved in something useful. My father picked me up at the station and took me back to my parents house. My mother was of course delighted to see me but the 9 o'clock news was showing on the TV and reports were just coming through that HMS *Sheffield* had been hit by an exocet missile, fired by an Argentine Super Etendard aircraft, causing an unknown loss of life and the remaining crew to abandon ship. Suddenly everything was put into perspective. My mother was not really impressed to hear I was going with the ship, even less so when I told her I had volunteered.

After a short four day, hectic leave (during which time I made a will for the very first time), I arrived back to the ship early on Sunday afternoon, to find that some bureaucratic cock up had placed my new berth down in a 1 deck cruise staff cabin which, although not in the pits, would not have been close enough to 'the boss'. Considering I was meant to be Jimmy's ADC, as it were, it wouldn't have been particularly handy. A few words in his ear and I shuffled off to meet Major Ron Cocking who, with his team of stalwarts, was in charge of the berthing arrangements. I ended up in 8101, a penthouse suite with a connecting staircase up to Jimmy's room. Never had I had such luxury, my only regret being that this trip was sure to be unaccompanied!

VIP visits.

Needless to say the next few days went extremely quickly, with total panic only being replaced by sheer desperation. The majority of the flight decks were in position, but a great deal of welding still had to take place. Workmen were scurrying around twenty four hours a day, achieving in hours what would normally have taken days, or even weeks - funny what happens when there is a certain amount of incentive.

My duties were to achieve solutions to the problems for the embarked Naval Party, Number 1980. Problems concerning the ship I knew intimately, and of which they knew very little. The officers soon knew enough though to make sure they were well ensconced in the top penthouse suites before the remainder of our 'guests' arrived. The navy do have this propensity of ensuring their own needs are met.

The one problem which was to add to our frustrations was that on sailing day, just about every member of the top brass was going to drop down to see the ship. We had to sort out some sort of schedule for them, ensuring they would be met, guided around the ship, taken to see the captain if required, etc. By this time Cunard's Senior Master, Captain Peter Jackson, had come back from leave and resumed command. I believe we had an Admiral, four Generals, including the Chief of the General Staff and followers, all arriving by helicopter. The large area on the other side of the Customs Shed, normally used for new cars in transit, was fast becoming Southampton's equivalent of Battersea Heliport.

They stayed for lunchtime cocktails with Captain Jackson in his cabin along with Ralph Bahna, Cunard Line's New York President, and Victor Mathews, the head of Trafalgar House, the group that owned Cunard Line.

The biggest panic was due to the arrival of John Nott, the Government Minister for Defence, who turned up at 1430 hours in yet another helicopter, along with the now infamous Ministry of Defence spokesman, Ian MacDonald, who was far from the somber person he appeared to be during his regular TV appearances. When I quizzed him as to this he was quite worried to think he was being depressing, in fact he had regularly caused great mirth in the Officers Wardroom. He told me that he had been instructed to talk faster, but he was apparently speaking to members of the press from all over the world, some of whom were not too brilliant with the English language, and therefore he didn't wish to be misquoted.

The Navy and Army had planned a route around the ship for John Nott so that he would be able to speak to some of the already embarked troops which numbered over three thousand. However, I believe he had no intention of being caught with any tricky questions and therefore moved as quickly as he thought reasonably possible. The route was soon covered so I led him to the bridge , allowing my fellow navigators their moment of glory.

We then worked our way back to the Midships Lobby via the now crowded boat deck. With half an hour before our scheduled sailing time, it seemed the total number of troops on board were hanging over the starboard side of the ship - and no wonder, there was a rather agile looking lady in some very interesting underwear delivering a singing telegram from the dockside, and yet another lady who decided to divest herself of some of her garments, much to the obvious pleasure of the lads!

The sailing.

Down below in the engine room all was not well. Only one of the three massive boilers used to provide steam for the turbines was on line. To make 29 knots the ship needed all three boilers, with two she could make about 21 knots, but with one we might make 5 or perhaps 7 knots and the ship would be most difficult to handle. The load from one boiler was mostly taken by the electrical requirements for the hotel side of the vessel.

Captain Peter Driver, our pilot was not a happy man. He knew the ship and understood the technical considerations which would affect the vessels handling, but to add to his problems there was a force 7 wind blowing and the QE2 is greatly affected by wind at slow speeds due to her high sides. The scheduled sailing time of 1600 Hours rapidly approached and literally the whole world was aware that the ships departure from Southampton, full of troops was imminent; if there was a delay it would not only be embarrassing, but the countries ability to achieve the great task ahead may be put in question - we simply had to sail!

During the past few days it had been decided that the ship would sail on two boilers (a fairly normal procedure) and the third would be put on line the next day. During the in port period one was in use to cover lighting, liquid pumping, galley and other hotel requirements while the other two would undergo routine maintenance. The day before had seen a second boiler flashed up and made ready for sailing, however a massive reserve feed distilled water leak was detected, a loss of nearly twenty tonnes per hour which could not be made up by the ship's own distillation plant.

The boiler feed water has to be exceedingly pure, less than four parts per million of contaminating solids are allowed, therefore the water is continually recirculated, and after it has been turned into steam and it's energy used, it is passed through a condenser which in turn is cooled by seawater. The problem was first considered to be a fractured tube in one of the boilers, this boiler was shut down for examination, a lengthy business which required allowing time for the boiler to cool down before the inspection could take place.

No leak could be found and the loss was still continuing. The same process had to be repeated with the other on line boiler and still the leak could not be found. Consequently when we came to sail only one boiler was back on line. The problem was not found until some time later; a forgotten valve had been opened and not closed.

A relatively minor problem such as lack of power was not going to change the minds of the powers that be, and by 1600 Hours the tugs had been made fast. The ropes and wires were taken in and the band started to play as the ship was slowly hauled from the quayside and into the river.

A tricky operation at the best of times, Captain Driver swung the ship perfectly off the old Ocean Terminal and we were pulled past thousands of relatives. Never have I seen so many people on the quay and never had I seen so many hanging over the ship's side; troops and crew everywhere, on the winches, by the rails, in the boats, penthouse balconies, even a couple on the forward crane. The engineers managed to give us sufficient power to make six knots with a tug pulling on the bow, a rather ignominious start but only realised by a few in the know. All the tugs except one were let go when the ship picked up speed and the final tug was not dismissed until we had navigated around the treacherous Brambles Bank, often the temporary resting place of large ships in the past.

Flying Stations.

We steamed slowly up the Eastern Solent, leaving Cowes and the Isle of Wight to starboard. The ship was brought to 'flying stations' for the first time and preparations were made to take on two Sea King helicopters of the newly formed 825 Squadron. They had come from the Royal Naval Air Station at Culdrose in Cornwall via RNAS Portland and were led by Lt. Commander Hugh Clark who was later to be awarded for bravery in the rescue of personnel from the fated *Sir Galahad.* Clark flew around the ship and then hovered to one side at the stern, 'exploring the envelope' I was told by Lt. Commander 'Tiger' Shaw, the officer in charge of flying for the embarked naval party. He was finding the areas around the flight deck which may be adversely affected by turbulence caused by the ship's superstructure and thus be a hazard to pilots landing on board.

He landed his aircraft, number 595, with the precision expected of a squadron commander. Within minutes the second Sea King, number 597, came into view, followed a similar maneuver and landed on the number three spot. The forward flight deck under the bridge was the number one spot, while the landing area aft were number two and three spots. After landing the rotors were automatically folded back, the machines rolled into their allotted parking place and secured down to the deck with the practiced efficiency of a well run team.

Captain Driver was disembarked once we had reached open water and the decision was made to anchor the vessel until a second boiler could be brought on line. We anchored at 2130 hours just three miles south of the Nab Tower off the east coast of the Isle of Wight. We often considered what the press would have made of the situation should they have found out. For the time being however, we took to the wardroom bar to chat about the days' most unusual events.

Rendezvous.

The next day brought better luck for the engineers; they had found their valve and just after 0900 hours, the *QE2* set sail again. We were to rendezvous, or RV as the Royal Navy say, with *Grey Rover*, a Royal Fleet Auxiliary tanker. A trial replenishment at sea (RAS) was to take place. One became accustomed, if not totally familiar with these endless abbreviations the Navy seemed to have.

The afternoon became a busy one. As we made our way down the English Channel it was reported that we had a soldier on board with a suspected appendicitis and it would be necessary to land him ashore. A little after five p.m. 'hands to flying stations' was piped. A little confusion became evident on the bridge as different messages were being received from the after deck. The patient was put on board the helicopter but it still did not take off. Eventually after a further twenty minutes, with the rotors turning, another patient was put aboard. A doctor, nurse and two patients left the ship at 1745 hours. Little Jane Yelland, one of our own nurses, came back a few hours later bubbling over as a result of her unexpected flight.

QE2 began to reduce speed for the RV, *Grey Rover* came up our starboard side from astern and a rocket line was fired across, to this was attached a heaving line, followed by another heavier line called a messenger. The two ships took up station about 150 feet apart and a distance line was secured between the two fo'cstles, with *Grey Rover* acting as the station keeper.

Approximately a hundred soldiers waited on 2 deck, by a door normally used for baggage which had become our RAS point. The men took up the slack in the messenger and commenced heaving in the eight inch flexible hose slung from the derricks of the tanker. With tremendous effort the end was brought aboard and coupled to a new bunker line which had been installed from the door, across the passenger alleyway, down the forward engine room escape and into the fuel reception tank. A few tonnes were pumped to test the line, the line then 'blown through' with compressed air to clear any oil residue and then disconnected. The operation proved a success and thus proved we could go south and refuel at sea if the need arose. The situation is one unusual for most navigators; the pressures involved between two ships in close proximity can quickly result in collision if sufficient concentration is not kept and is therefore one we don't, as a rule, practice.

Grey Rover retrieved her hose and the two ships separated with the sound of three long blasts on the whistle, the sailors salute.

In the meantime helicopter 595 was sitting at Trelisk Hospital near Truro in Cornwall. Apparently the Doctor and nurse were causing minor chaos by attempting to purloin the daily papers from wherever they could lay their hands. They finally returned just after 2000 hours and the ship turned towards the Bay of Biscay two hours later, the business of getting our troops to their destination was now our priority.

Drill !

The *Queen* headed for Freetown in Sierra Leone, a voyage of almost 3000 miles and during the next few days we settled into the routine of being at sea. The normal shipping lanes were avoided to prevent visual detection. The Navy expected Soviet surveillance of one type or another but to our knowledge none came, although we were buzzed by a French *'Atlantic'* class reconnaissance plane, the pilot of which came over the radio and wished us well.

The first emergency drill for the troops was on Thursday, a 'find your way around drill'; Fridays' was to be more comprehensive. First Officer Bob Hayward and I had a lengthy conversation as to how we should run the drill - there were many problems to overcome. The twenty lifeboats could not take all crew and passengers so extra liferafts had been put on board to compensate. We first intended that the normal procedure of passengers following the coloured arrows to their muster stations as indicated in their cabins should occur, but the sheer volume of troops at each muster station was staggering. Cabins intended for two now had three or four in, with men using collapsible camp beds.

I had explained to Regimental Sergeant Major Hunt, a little man with a big voice, our plan to get the men to their stations and divide them into groups of twenty five. Confusion reigned the first day, but gradually things became sorted. Each muster station had an Officer or NCO in charge and each group of twenty five had a designated leader. Four of the ships' deck officers went around on Friday and spoke to each muster station group in turn, explaining what we expected of them and that should an emergency arise, they would be led either to a boat or raft which would have already been swung out into the embarkation position by the ships' crew.

All were quite receptive and the troops organised themselves well. It had been my intention to take the onus from us and put it into their own hands as in a real emergency we might be busy elsewhere. The Gurkhas, the little soldiers from Nepal, were the best, actually disciplining themselves to form tight groups, sitting down cross legged and silent when all were present. The officers were quite amusing, they seemed to stand uneasily at their muster point, waiting for leadership, which Sergeant Major Cocking soon gave! One young Captain thought it would be better if he mustered with his 'boys' - I respectfully pointed out to him that we would not be holding hands when we got into the lifeboats.

The drills soon worked well and over the next few days we took the group leaders and gave them instruction on the techniques required to launch the boats and rafts and basics lessons on survival; not surprisingly they were very attentive.

Daily routines.

The army devised an impressive timetable to cope with the 3000 plus troops, so divided that small groups of men could be seen anywhere at any time, in alleyways, lounges, recesses, stairwells, etc., learning to take their firearms apart and put them back together - blindfolded, first aid, enemy aircraft recognition. Some would be jogging around the boat deck, later with full kit and back pack with firearms, and sometimes carrying each other. PT was a regular occurrence on the outside decks. The swimming pools were used on a rota basis throughout the day.

The Gurkhas amazed us on Saturday morning. They had been allocated cabins on 5 deck as these were low down in the ship and thought to be more suitable as the men were known to be prone to seasickness. These cabins were furthest from the boat stations and their British officers decided the troops should practice their escape blindfolded, which might simulate the effect should the power fail and the lighting be extinguished. Consequently odd groups of ten or twenty could be seen at varying times of the day groping around passageways and up the stairs. A certain amount of amusement was guaranteed when one became lost and found staggering around the tables in the restaurant!

Fire arms practice commenced from the flight decks, we had loaded a considerable amount of 'ready use' ammunition for this purpose. An officer was posted on the bridge to ensure firing was halted should we come within range of other vessels. There was a large variety of weapons being carried including sub machine guns, self loading rifles, shoulder held anti tank weapons and 'blow pipe' anti aircraft missiles. Needless to say that some of the watchkeepers found it difficult to sleep with the staccato sound of firing being heard at odd times during the day. Target practice often meant firing at bags of rubbish deliberately thrown over the side and frequently the nets surrounding the flight deck were shot away. The ship still had a stanchion on the fo'cstle with a shell hole many years later.

Flying Practice.

Flying practice took place in earnest from Friday onwards for two or three hours a day. The Navy were still unaware of how or where the troops would be taken off the ship, although it was anticipated that they may have to be transferred by helicopter while the ship was underway. Many of the young pilots had never flown on or off a ship before and consequently they needed to practice the maneuvers involved, to find the areas around the ship to avoid and the correct angle of approach.

In the event of a two spot operation taking place at the after flight deck, the pilots would have to fly on and off the forward spot, number 2, in an athwartships direction while the after spot, number 3, would involve flying fore and aft, or in the direction of the ships travel. To land on a heaving deck in rough rainy weather with a ship, making twenty five knots, seemed difficult enough, landing sideways would take considerable skill. The pilot has to approach the ship using part of the vessel as a fixed visual reference, his eyes telling his brain that the ship is stationary and that it is the water below that is moving. He must be flying sideways at twenty five knots and it is the thrust given by the tail rotor which is the deciding factor as to whether he can maintain his direction and position.

During these flying operations the bridge was a busy place and the 'yes' or 'no' for landings and take off's were given by 'Tiger' Shaw. He was fed information direct from the Flight Deck Officer, Roger Bevan, via a rating stationed with a talk back system on the port side of the wheelhouse, and also from a naval Petty Officer who sat at one of the ship's radars, adapted to receive signals from the helicopter transponder. He was also in direct communication with both helicopters via VHF radio. The business was very intense and there was little time for our sometimes frivolous comments regarding their 'paraffin pigeons'

Throughout all their operations the Navy had great respect for our ship and at all times showed courtesy and professionalism.

Freetown.

On Tuesday 18th May, at 0800 Hours, the bridge gave the engine room one and a half hours notice for our arrival at Freetown. The call was made solely for the purpose of replenishing our tanks with fuel and water and it would be the last time the ship would be secured alongside till our return to Southampton over three weeks later.

I had been to Freetown several times before during my employment with Palm Line, a British cargo shipping company trading with the west coast of Africa. The last occasion was almost five years previously while

65

serving on the *Matadi Palm,* a 14,000 tonne deadweight vegetable oil carrier.

Two harbour pilots boarded at the fairway buoy and assisted the Captain with their local knowledge. They appeared highly qualified as they had more gold braid on their shoulders than most of the other officers on the bridge, although on one, this air of respectability was somewhat dulled by his sickly green coloured shoes with enormous heels, (the latter presumably fitted so that he could see over the bridge dodger!) a sight which kept us amused for some time.

By 1145 hours the ship had been secured to the Queen Elizabeth II quay. We had traveled 2956 miles in a little over five days, making an average speed of 24.35 Knots and consuming 1919 tonnes of heavy oil fuel. Shore leave was not granted and only the agent came aboard, a few people came inquisitively around the dock and one or two expatriates came past in their speed boats, Union Jacks patriotically flying. The usual 'bum' boats came and sent their lines aboard to peddle their wares. We were also passed by a Soviet trawler which seemed to have one or two aerials too many. We had been expecting sooner or later to be detected by one of their spy trawlers known as Alien Intelligence Gatherers. (AIG)

Ascension Island.

A film was being shown on deck as we pulled away from Freetown around 2300 hours. There were few people on the dock to witness our departure. 1867 tonnes of fuel had been pumped on board. The pilots disembarked before midnight and the vessel set a course for the island of Ascension, the small outcrop of British sovereignty deep in the South Atlantic near the equator.

The Admiralty had informed Captain James not to go within twenty five miles of the island. We presumed to avoid any unneccessary detection and reporting to the 'other side' of our intentions or whereabouts and it was much to Captain James's annoyance therefore when a Soviet AIG approached on Thursday morning. The small ship took a good look and then departed.

We made a rendesvous with HMS *Dumbarton Castle*, the navy's latest patrol craft designed for North Sea oil protection duties. One of our Sea Kings was launched at 1330 hours and despatched towards the island. Less than an hour later a yellow Sea King of the RAF headed towards the ship, looking rather out of place away from the UK coast where it's prime duties were that of air-sea recue. By 1500 hours the Sea Kings were operating a shuttle service between the *QE2* and the warship which by now was keeping station off our starboard side, transfering stores and personnel. By 1600 hours flying was completed for the day, but we had to keep within the area in readyness for the arrival of General Moore and his command staff who were flying out from the UK that night. This was the night of the 20th and, unknown to us, the next day was to be the occasion when British troops would land at San Carlos on East Falkland.

Flying commenced in earnest early the next day to transfer stores and mail destined for other ships in the task force, including the STUFT ships, 'Ships taken up from trade'. Three Sea Kings, two Wessex and one Chinook helicopter were used to carry underslung loads and more troops, including General Moore. The General was allotted what was normally the most expensive accommodation on board, the 'Queen Mary Suite'.

Some very impressive flying was seen that day with, at times, up to three 'helos' stacked up astern waiting to come in and drop their load, over 200 tonnes of stores were loaded. The forward spot in front of the bridge, number 1, was also used at times, but only by the RAF Sea King pilot who seemed to be unconcerned by the fact that as he hovered athwartships just above the deck, there was 67,000 tonnes of ocean splendor rushing towards him at 18 knots. From the bridge we could look down directly into his cockpit, he also showed great skill in coming down aft and putting the underslung load onto the after deck as the ship was skidding around in a 180o turn.

The pilot of the large twin rotored Chinook also showed us his impressive flying prowess at the end of the day by hovering level with the port bridge wing for several minutes, his crew seemed to be poking their heads out of every window plus the tailgate taking photographs. He turned his aircraft through 90o and flew sideways facing the bridge and matched our forward speed for a few minutes before he left. We continued our southerly progress.

After General Moore and his officers boarded we became tight on space, I was the only officer other than 'Jimmy' James with a single cabin. Needless to say I had to move and found myself in suite 8002 sharing with 'Tiger' Shaw and Roger Bevan. The room had two beds which folded away during the day so it was not really an inconvenience, but I received a certain amount of ribbing from my fellow officers in the wardroom.

We did have a few laughs together. Every evening before going to take a shower Roger would imitate Major Hugh Afleck Graves, whose voice was almost as 'far back' as his name. Afleck-Graves was responsible for coordinating the troop disembarkation and would muster the men by announcing "Assault stations, assault stations, groups so and so proceed to assault station now" After a while this broadcast would send everyone into fits of laughter and Roger would announce to the cabin before he went to take a shower "Ablution stations, ablution stations, stand by to ablute!"

Throughout the voyage south we were following the *Baltic Ferry* and her sister ship *Nordic Ferry* who were about a day or so ahead. Behind was the *Atlantic Causeway,* sister ship to the ill fated *Atlantic Conveyor.* All these ships had equipment belonging to our passengers, the 5th Infantry Brigade, as well as more helicopters and pilots of 825 Squadron. We did send a helicopter over to *Causeway* the day after we left Ascension to pick up important equipment and on that afternoon a Wessex helicopter arrived unexpectantly with further stores.

Blackout.

Captain James was under instruction to black the ship out and preparations were made after we left Freetown; I was given the task of supervising the operation. We had to change the *QE2* from being 'the brightest star on the ocean to the darkest' said 'Jimmy' when he addressed the crew. There are of course many hundreds of portholes and windows on the ship. Bill Bailey and his team of four carpenters cut out templates for the different sizes and I think thousands of pieces of black plastic were cut. Each deck became the responsibility of one or two army officers and the troops were given large amounts of masking tape to complete the job. The large windows in the ship's side were given to fatigue parties and the whole exercise was completed in three days.

In the tropics the sun caused the black plastic to heat up and crinkle, it also resulted in the ship becoming much warmer.

I was able to take a helicopter trip one evening when the flight crews were commencing their night flying exercises. From a mile away it was difficult to spot the ship even though the blackout was not fully complete. Except for a few areas not yet covered, only the navigation lights were visible and these were not used after we left Ascension. The effect was rather ghostly and surreal, most impressive.

We darkened ship at sunset, checked as best we could from the overhanging bridge wings and also by clambering around the lifeboats to check some of the penthouse suites whose occupants were at times a little forgetful.

The blackout routine spoilt the party Brigadier Tony Wilson intended to have on deck. Instead he transferred the venue to the 'Q4 Room', the ship's nightclub and continued with the entertainment which included ten minutes of Gurkha bagpipes, followed by the pipes and drums of the Welsh Guards and the bagpipe band of the Scots Guards. Very entertaining but somewhat hard on the ears in that relatively small room.

The reports of attacks.

Captain James and Brigadier Wilson gave a brief lecture to the ships' crew in the theater in order to pass on what information was possible regarding the task ahead. They explained the problems and dangers and thanked the crew as they were the only ones on board who had actually volunteered to take the voyage.

There was much interest shown in the broadcasts made by the World Service of the BBC. Unconfirmed reports were made on the evening of the 22nd that a landing had been made at San Carlos. These were confirmed shortly after by information coming into the military satellite equipment which had been set up on board. Most disturbing was the news that the Argentine Air Force were making successful bombing attacks on our ships and of the loss of HMS *Ardent* and HMS *Antelope*.

Then came news of the attacks on HMS *Coventry* and *Atlantic Conveyor.* The latter was a ship belonging to the cargo division of Cunard and was particularly bad news for those who had either worked on board or knew men there. We also considered the affect this information would have on our families at home, who would be party to less information regarding our well being than we knew ourselves.

The days of sailing south continued, flying operations carried on, blackout was enforced and extra lookouts were posted with machine guns. Large bren guns were mounted on platforms on either bridge wing and test firing was carried out with their five inch ammunition - very noisy! The watertight doors were closed at night as the possibility of submarine attack was considered possible by the Navy. Radios and radars were kept switched off to prevent our position being obtained by their transmission.

On the 26th we commenced evasive steering; the weather was deteriorating as we sailed further into the southern winter. The visibility reduced and on the morning of the 27th, First Officer Bob Hayward decided it would be more prudent to have the radar on, a fortuitous decision. The ship had entered a field of large glacial icebergs and the radar showed them both behind and ahead. Captain Jackson took over the con and for the next six hours the ship was navigated with caution, deviating from its intended course to avoid the large bergs. When dawn broke we were rewarded with the spectacular sight of huge bergs visible above the mists, the sunrise creating wonderful shades of red, orange and yellow to be reflected from the normal blue-white ice.

We passed one berg which we calculated to be over a mile long and three hundred feet high, we altered course to give it a wide berth and the mists came down and enveloped it like a shroud., it's ghostly shape hardly visible beneath.

HMS Antrim.

Captain James received instruction to rendesvous with HMS *Antrim*. General Moore and his staff of about forty were to be transferred so that he could quickly catch up with Admiral Sandy Woodward and the British troops which had landed and were now setting up defensive positions at base camp near San Carlos Water. *Antrim* had been having similar problems with ice, but the rendesvous went ahead on schedule, they had known our position from the moment our radars had been switched on.

The decision had been made to transfer most of the men by our own Harding launches as the sea conditions were slight except for a fairly large swell. General Moore went over by helicopter and, even though the Sea King was considered normally too large to land on that deck, the pilot managed by landing at 45 degrees, thus enabling all three sets of wheels to touch - a difficult operation considering the swell.

The swell was also to make the boat transfer more hazardous than expected, several attempts had to be made before all had embarked onto Antrim. One Junior Army Officer however, was not quite agile enough; as he jumped for the rope ladder hanging from the warship he was caught between the two as the swell lifted the launch and trapped his leg. He was lifted to the deck, diagnosed and immediately put on the helicopter to be returned to the QE2 where our hospital took care of him.

Antrim had already seen action, both in South Georgia and East Falkland, the evidence was visible by her somewhat weather beaten exterior but also by the line of canon shell holes down her side. Her 'Seacat' missile launcher was out of action as the result of an unexploded bomb which had lodged itself in the magazine and fortunately been defused before it could explode and remove the stern of the vessel.

South Georgia.

By 1330 Hours we were on our way, our instructions were to make for South Georgia. The fog was still present and we could see nothing when 'stand by' was rung at 1745 Hours. I made my way forward to supervise the letting go of the anchor. Because of the new flight deck, just getting forward was a little precarious, I had to virtually swing over the ship's side to get there. The two carpenters who operate the controls of the anchor windlass were all but hidden from me by the tons of steel, and we had to communicate by walkie-talkie - or bellow at the top of our voices.

Captain Jackson brought the ship into Cumberland Bay, navigating through the fog by radar. On the fo'cstle we walked the anchor back to two shackles in the water, 180 feet of the chain was below the surface. The reason for this was because the bay was very deep and if we had let go 'from the pipe', the anchor and cable would race down to the ocean floor and the momentum would bring the remainder out of the cable locker and probably cause considerable damage.

I peered through the murk at the water, black as the blackest night - I could see nothing except the gentlest ripple as the stem cut through the water way below me as we crept gently into the bay. The bridge was invisible behind me, a rather un-nerving experience considering the circumstances of our position. When the Captain had decided on his anchor position the engines were put astern and then I could not detect the ship's forward momentum through the water, just feel a slight vibration under my feet as the propellers brought the 67,000 tonnes to a halt.

The wash made by the astern movement gradually came forward, I could see the discharged water from the galleys coming towards the bow. When the order was given the carpenters opened the brake of the windlass and the anchor cable dropped away with increasing speed, the anchor hit the bottom as the 5th shackle raced over the gypsy, the carpenters struggled with the brake trying to slow the progress of the cable which was now jumping along the rollers and down the hawse pipe bringing mud, rust and sparks up from the chain locker. I darted for the port side in attempt to miss the 'bitter end' should it part from it's securing point in the locker - to my great relief they brought the rushing chain to a halt with only two shackles left on board.

The *QE2* anchored at 1922 hours, approximately one mile from the old whaling station at Gritvigen. The passage from Freetown had taken eight days, twenty hours and twelve minutes, a distance of 5035 miles, consumed 3570 tonnes of fuel at an average speed of 23.9 knots.

The ferry *Norland* and the P & O liner *Canberra* were already at anchor and a meeting took place soon after our arrival with the Senior Naval Officers and Captain Barker from HMS *Endurance,* which was also anchored in the bay. The troops were to disembark immediately into requisitioned trawlers and be transferred to *Norland* and *Canberra.* The delay in transferring troops would therefore be minimal, the discharge of stores and ammunition would be more time consuming. These would be transferred to the Fleet Auxiliary ship *Stromness* which would be arriving the next day with the survivors of HMS *Coventry.*

Disembarkation.

HMS *Leeds Castle,* sister to *Dumbarton Castle* was the first vessel to try and come alongside in the late evening darkness, her lights only becoming visible as she closed to one hundred feet. Her mast hit our bridge wing extensions as she tried to maneuver under number one hatch, and she had to move away.

The *Cordella* then was the first to secure alongside. She was one of five North Sea trawlers which had been taken up from trade, she and the others, *Northella, Farnella, Junella* and *Pict* made up the newly formed 11th Mine Countermeasures Squadron. They were manned with Royal Navy Officers and ratings to act as mine sweepers in the waters off the Falkland Islands. Except for paintwork, and a ships pontoon which shouldn't have been down, very little damage was done in bringing these large vessels alongside, their new Commanders showing considerable skill.

The transfer went on throughout the night, the trawlers making repeated journeys over to *Canberra,* or unloading stores from number one hatch forward. The Admiralty salvage tug *Typhoon* was also utilised to take troops to the *Norland.*

The following morning I woke to see a hive of activity. Meanwhile the fog had become very patchy and one of the most remarkable vistas in my experience was visible. South Georgia is a land of tall rugged mountains reaching up towards 10,000 feet and in every valley there appears to be a glacier, Hamberg, Harker and Nordenfjold Glaciers could all be seen from our anchorage. Nestling between these barren peaks was Grytviken, a deserted whaling station of rusted iron and dilapidated wooden buildings. Through the binoculars the conning tower of the crippled Argentine submarine Santa Fe could be made out lying at an angle against the old wooden jetty. The wreck of an Argentinean helicopter was on the hillside above King Edward Cove.

In the foreground lay *Canberra* looking slightly worse for wear with rust streaking her side; she had already been in the firing line at San Carlos. *Norland* lay astern of us looking very far away from home in the North Sea. Flying commenced a little after eight as soon as the fog lifted sufficiently for us to be able to see the other ships, then went on throughout the day with stores being lifted from our forward flight deck. The 'wasp' helicopter from *Endurance* flew on with their Captain and a number of conferences seemed to take place. On board *QE2* Lieutenant Commander David Poole, our Executive Officer, took charge of the transfer operation assisted by the Navigator from *Endurance.*

During the morning it became evident that we may not get all the troops off within the prepared schedule; a worried looking officer from the 7th Gurkha asked if we could use one or two of the ship's own Harding launches to transfer his men. I assisted by starting to load up these tiny men just before midday, along with their equipment which appeared more than they could physically carry. Upon reaching *Norland* we realised that they had no pontoon for us to come alongside, only a shell door opening some eight feet above the water, normally used for the loading and discharge of vehicles. The

Gurkhas could not even see over it yet alone climb through it, but we brought the boat alongside and by using the roof of the boat's cab plus a good shove from behind we managed to safely embark them all. I was sorry to see them go, these little men had been courteous, obedient and efficient.

The Chief Officer of *Norland* dropped down onto the boat and talked of his recent experiences with the ship at San Carlos Water, the area now referred to as 'Bomb Alley'. He told me that he had been on the port bridge wing when an Argentine *'Mirage'* fighter had flown past beneath him and a *'Skyhawk'* had been shot down by soldiers lying on their backs using their sub-machine guns. Another *'Skyhawk'* was 'splashed' by a British missile, hit over their heads, parts of plane falling all around them. There was a line of cannon shell holes along one section of the side similar to HMS *Antrim*.

On our return journey to the *QE2* we carried some of the survivors from HMS *Ardent;* they looked a pathetic sight as few of them had their own clothing - what they wore was mostly borrowed with their few personal belongings in plastic bags. Even though they looked a shambles they did not look defeated, but there was no lighthearted banter.

By 1655 Hours, when darkness had returned, all flying had ceased and our two helicopters with their crew were embarked onto *Canberra*. The troops had gone and by the next morning so had *Canberra* and *Norland*.

The weather had remained settled with only light airs, the temperature had stayed between 0o C and 3.1o C. The overcast skies had ensured that we were not visible from above, consequently our greatest hazard could have come from one of the few German built submarines which the Navy knew the Argentineans had in service. The QE2 would have presented an admirable target while at anchor at the head of the bay and this was possibly the most dangerous period of our voyage.

Ashore in Grytviken.

Throughout Friday night stores were continually being transferred into the trawlers, these were stores for which *Canberra* could not be held back and were therefore later loaded onto *Stromness*.

Afleck-Graves had been liaising with the Commanding Officer ashore where approximately one hundred troops were now based in the British Antarctic Survey Base, close to the old whaling station. On Saturday morning one of our boats was put down and thirty of our people headed for the shore. The closer we came, the more desperate the landscape looked and this dilapidated, forgotten little cluster of buildings appeared more like a wild west ghost town than anything I had seen before.

The temperature was colder inshore as the boat pushed it's way through the brash ice and the mountains looked daunting in their numerous shades of somber grey and black flecked with the white of snow drifts and hanging mist.

We were met by one of the Army Officers who had been with the troops which had retaken the island a few weeks before. He had the cold hard look of the SAS professional, a serious man who I don't recall smiling throughout our visit. Our landing was at the old wooden pier near the submarine *Santa Fe* and he advised us not to poke around on our own, there was a possibility of Argentine booby traps still as yet undiscovered.

We passed the submarine, its conning tower lying at an angle away from the jetty. Crudely painted on the side in large white letters was the message "Keep Off, by order of the Commanding Officer *Endurance*" - as though coach loads of tourists would appear at any moment, or perhaps it was meant for the more light fingered, souvenir hunting soldier based at the camp. Two whalers lay partly sunk in shallow water close by, just abandoned when the last men left in the early 60's. The fresh snow lay on the rotting jetty where odd boards were broken or missing; the impression was that we were the first people to arrive for twenty years.

The other buildings around were factory units, offices, dormitories and even a church, all made from timber and looking similar to the houses found in the Norwegian countryside, except the paintwork was faded and chipped, doors were ajar, windows were dirty and broken. The steelwork and galvanized iron sheeting of the working areas had rusted and collapsed over the years giving an air of decay.

We followed in the Officer's footsteps, passing two soldiers about to start a week's patrol. The garrison was split roughly into two with half on patrol for a week, sleeping in bivouacs, while the others were back at base. They were equipped with the usual sort of armaments and also VHF radios with headsets around their helmets. We went around the factory with it's whale oil tanks, part of the processing plant.

Paul Guest, the ship's photographer, and I held back to take a few photographs while the others proceeded into an old wooden church, complete with steeple. Quite suddenly we were surprised to hear the sound of an organ coming from the white building. We followed inside to find that one the Second Officers, Chris Haughton, had found this wonderful old organ on the inside balcony. With some little persuasion and hefty pumping he managed to play the first few bars of Bach's Toccata and Fugue in 'D', The church, was not in fact as dilapidated as the other buildings and had been in regular use by the Antarctic Survey and latterly by the army.

We continued our trek through the old whaling station, seeing old tools, lathes and other machinery which looked as though it had been left one Friday night prior to a weekend off. One old whaler was still afloat at another jetty and, except for it's rusty and unused appearance, it looked as though it could be made seaworthy.

Our path took us out of town, past the derelict hulk of an old sailing ship long since beached and with only one mast remaining in place, to a tiny cemetery where about thirty graves could be identified. Here lies the grave of Sir Earnest Shackleton, the Antarctic explorer whose perilous journey across the Southern Ocean to South Georgia is recalled in Frank Wordsley's 'Shackleton's Boat Journey'. Wordsley was his Captain on the *Endurance*.

There was also a new grave in the cemetery, that of Victorio Artuso, the Argentine submariner who was unfortunately killed after the island was recaptured. The story we were told was that the submarine was being moved to the jetty under escort, Artuso was shot when he reached up to adjust a ballast valve, the guard believing an act of sabotage was about to take place. His grave was marked with a simple polished wooden cross with his name and the date.

We made our way back to the launch, some of the lads picking up old whale bones and harpoon heads for souvenirs, in the distance *QE2* looked surreal in the mists. Another boat followed us back, full of troops from the base, coming out to sample briefly the comparative luxury of the ship.

Departure Grytviken.

During that afternoon stores continued to be discharged, however, the weather was changing quickly, the barometer was falling and the wind picking up. The sea was being whipped up and the increasing swell coming through the entrance of the bay was causing the ship to yaw uncomfortably which in turn made the trawlers alongside heave unpredictably.

Captain James had a report that the tanker *British Wye* was being bombed by an unidentified aircraft just four hundred miles to the north. He assumed the Argentines could therefore reach our position and decided that we should leave, even though munitions were still in the hold.

All the survivors from the attacked warships *Ardent, Antelope* and *Coventry* were safely aboard and at 1727 hours the anchor was raised and we steamed out of the bay, increasing speed to 18 knots and heading east. By 1930 Hours we were back in the ice field and Captain Jackson maneuvered his ship through the many bergs which in the darkness could only be seen on the radar, assuming the ice would also make detection difficult for the Argentinean forces. By 2200 we had cleared the ice field and speed was increased to 25 knots and the course to 045o.

Journey north.

The following morning Captain James chaired his usual nine o'clock meeting with two of the Executive Officers from the warships, the third had not survived his ship's attack and his place had been taken by another officer. All three were not comfortable and were obviously still suffering some degree of shock from their experience under fire. They did seem however to be attempting to give the impression of a brave front and continue life as normal. Discipline and ship routine would continue with each of the vessels treating themselves as a separate unit.

I raised the matter of boat drill and explained this would occur for the survivors during the morning. There were only approximately 650 men, therefore the routine should be that much simpler than before, however I was questioned in great detail about our procedures. They were very anxious as previous experiences had proved that plans prepared on paper do not always follow the way expected in practise. One of the men believed that the crews should muster below the level of the lowest aluminium deck as it had been proved that aluminium burns extremely well after being hit by an 'exocet' missile. I had to point out that in a ship of our size this would be extremely impracticable and that at least they should try our well proven method. The drill was practised and found to be satisfactory except I found the Navy ratings seemed a little less disciplined that the men of the army - a holiday mood had set in.

After leaving the bumpy waters of South Georgia the weather gradually improved and as we proceeded northwards the sun appeared and the pensive mood on board began to lift. The blackout procedure and radio silence continued although messages via the satellite equipment could still be sent and received.

Rendesvous with *Bayleaf.*

Only 886 tonnes of fuel remained on board by Tuesday 1st June, enough only for another day and a half steaming. A rendesvous was scheduled with the new Fleet Auxiliary ship *Bayleaf* and by late afternoon we had reduced speed to keep station with the oiler. The sea however was considered to rough, the wind was force 8 from the west north west and the *QE2* was rolling moderately to a rough sea and heavy swell.

The weather had moderated only slightly by the next morning, but the refueling had to proceed. *Bayleaf* approached up our starboard side and a fuel line was connected just after 0900 hours; the ships were only 150 feet apart and the sea between was being whipped up as both vessels rolled in the heavy swell. *Bayleaf* was shipping spray over her fore deck and rolling through 40 degrees or more. Captain Jackson watched apprehensively from the bridge wing as the operation continued and the oiler kept station with the *QE2,* a role reversal for the Royal Fleet Auxiliary. We continued on a course of 300 degrees, the pipeline heaved and fell and at times looked as though it would part, awful grating noises could be heard coming from the shell door recess where the hose was connected.

Bunkering was finally completed shortly after 1830 hours and the pipelines were disconnected, possibly only just in time, as the joining shackle which supported the block which in turn supported the fuel oil hose was found to be almost worn through from the constant chafing - it could have parted at any time.

Bayleaf cleared away by 1850 hours, we had been steaming in tandem for almost ten hours and bunkered 3834 tonnes of fuel, a remarkable achievement and a creditable performance by all the navy men involved.

Entertainment.

The continued involvement of the *QE2* in this war was still uncertain. We expected our passengers would disembark at Ascension Island and that the ship would proceed south again. The Navy decided to put on a show and in a few short days managed to find more 'acts' than they could cope with. The performance was extremely funny, most professional and of course quite crude at times, as can be expected from sailors. Our ladies from the laundry, who had replaced the normal Chinese laundrymen on board, were given front row seats and enjoyed every minute. The Double Down Show Room was alive with the spirit of these brave men who had come from the very front of battle, when at the end they sung 'God Save the Queen' the atmosphere was one of great emotion.

A few nights later on the 3rd of June, a Naval Mess Dinner was given in the Princess Grill by the Officers of the sunken ships and Naval Party 1980 for the Officers from the wardroom of the *QE2*. There were a couple of patriotic speeches, but the dinner was unusual in that the survivors were wearing a hodge podge of borrowed shirts, epaulettes and other clothing, not the blue 'mess' that the navy wore for these normally formal occasions.

The spirit and fervor was maintained after dinner by returning to the Queens Grill Bar where 'traditional mess games' were to take place. In my capacity as liaison officer I felt it my duty to provide whatever accompaniments were deemed necessary and these included two dozen empty wine bottles and a dozen broom handles. Balancing on an upturned wine bottle and attempting to dismount your similarly handicapped opponent using a broomstick is a tricky and dangerous operation - the shins suffering the most from repeated blows.

Tug of war using a broomstick in place of a rope is another popular 'pastime' on these occasions, with both teams squatting on the deck holding onto each other. The game is equally uncivilised, the aim being to win by fair means or foul.

New Orders.

Our new orders arrived. It had been decided that the *QE2* would return to Southampton via Ascension and not return to the south. Many of us felt initially disappointed because compared to *Canberra* we had done very little so far, however, we came to realise that much had in fact been achieved and the transport of the troops would prove to be invaluable in shortening the process of war in the Falklands.

On Friday 4th. June we were to rendesvous again with *Dumbarton Castle* off Ascension Island to transfer stores and personnel, including two casualties and six SAS men, the survivors of the helicopter crash that killed nineteen of their comrades. They were a very private group who kept themselves to themselves and wanted to be lifted off the ship before we reached Southampton and thus avoid any publicity or welcoming committee. One of the injured was the helicopter pilot, he had broken his foot in pushing his way out through the nearest window after the helicopter had crashed into the sea and turned over. His action had saved the lives of those who would otherwise have died, but he was at first uncomfortable with his memories. We managed to bring him around during the remainder of the voyage by including him in our more sociable activities plus generous quantities of alcohol.

The transfer was complete within four hours and by 1830 we were back up to full speed and heading a course for the United Kingdom.

The return.

The final days passed quickly as preparations were made to return to Southampton. A reception committee was expected and we would pass the Royal Yacht *Brittania* on our way up the Solent. A decision was made to re-kit the navy survivors before arrival, consequently on the afternoon of Thursday June 10th 'hands to flying stations' was piped again. Helicopters from RNAS Culdrose in Cornwall flew out to meet us off Mounts Bay, bringing stores and a few important people, one of whom was to tell us what we could and could not say to the press. The SAS members left and overnight we proceeded up the channel at slow speed.

The timetable for Friday had been carefully planned with our arrival at the Needles pilot station around 0845 hours. Earlier in the morning Admiral Sir John Fieldhouse was to join by helicopter accompanied by Lord Mathews. They went around the ship talking to the sailors before holding a press conference in the Q4 Room, which I had to introduce and give my version of events, with the forty media that had also arrived by 'chopper' off Portland.

Captain Driver boarded at 0848 hours and we proceeded up the Needles Channel, past the western end of the Isle of Wight. The survivors lined up on the starboard side of the flight decks on this beautiful June morning. As we slowly passed the Royal Yacht they gave three cheers to Her Majesty The Queen Mother who waved graciously from the after deck of Brittania. She sent this telegram to Captain Jackson,

"I am pleased to welcome you back as QE2 returns to home waters after your tour of duty in the South Atlantic. The exploits of your own ship's company and the deeds of valor of those who served in 'Antelope', 'Coventry' and 'Ardent' have been acclaimed throughout the land and I am proud to add my personal tribute'.

We proceeded up Southampton Water surrounded by dozens of small boats while helicopters and planes flew overhead. As we passed the oil refinery at Fawley each ship lying alongside signaled a salute and filled the air with a cacophony of whistles. On the dock hundreds of people were visible all waving flags and banners.

The ship turned off the berth and by the time we approached the quay the cheering and shouts were even louder than the marine band playing in front of the terminal. Everywhere there seemed to be cameras and press; when I went through the wardroom the whole spectacle was being shown live on T.V.

A red carpet had been prepared and was placed as soon as the gangway was in position; the survivors were ushered ashore to be met by a host of senior Naval Officers and local dignitaries applauding, each was given a red rose. They were, I'm sure, surprised by the reception and perhaps a little bemused by it all, but the main intention was to reunite them with their families as soon as possible and a secluded area in the terminal had been set aside, away from the prying eyes of public and media.

The crew of the *QE2* meanwhile started to file ashore from the forward gangway; it became almost impossible to move with hundreds of emotional, but happy relatives all gathered around. A very special day for us all.

PostScript.

The conversion of the ship back to its original condition took considerably longer than its conversion to a troop ship. While the helicopter decks were removed Cunard took the opportunity to complete much other work which included changing the Q4 Room into the Club Lido, one of the inside pool areas into a spa with Jacuzzis and repainting the dark blue hull a light grey. Survey work intended to be completed at the next scheduled refit was finished and the ship eventually left Southampton on August 14th, making her way to New York where a huge welcome awaited her.

Queen Elizabeth 2 achieved a new following by being at the forefront of the world news and the relatively short period 'at war' ensured her continued success as the most famous ocean liner in service.

QUOTES.

From **The Daily Mail,** 20th May, by Ross Mark in Washington.

*"The Soviet Union has deployed two spy satellites to pinpoint the **Queen Elizabeth 2** for air and submarine attack, according to the authoritative 'Aerospace Daily'.*
American intelligence sources confirm that at least some of the twelve Soviet radar, photographic and communication satellites are being used in the hunt for the liner.
*- Former American Chief of Naval Operations, Admiral Elmo Zumwalt said in a television interview he expected Argentina to make an effort to destroy the **QE2** by air and submarine attacks. "It is one big fat target", the Admiral said.".*

From **5th. Infantry Brigade/QE2 News,** 20th May 1982, on board.

"Gurkha soldiers have difficulty saying 'General Galtiere', instead they have come up with the name 'General Galti Gare', as well as being easier to say, this name is actually most appropriate. It means 'The General who made a mistake'."

From **5th. Infantry Brigade/QE2 News,** 26th May 1982, on board.

" *A message from the Commander, M.J.A. Wilson. Brigadier - "Very shortly we shall all transfer to other ships off South Georgia and start the last phase of our move to the Falkland Islands. It looks as if the Brigade will be there about 1st June, that is early next week.*

Once there, we shall join 3 Commando Brigade, We shall sort ourselves out; and then start joint operations to recapture the Islands.

Orders will be given out on landing; it is too early yet to issue a detailed plan, for it would be bound to change over the course of the next five days.

*This is the final issue of this newspaper, and to the Master and ship's company of **QE2** I would say 'Thank you for the way you have looked after us on this voyage. We have come to know you well, we admire you, and we shall always be proud that we sailed with you in your magnificent ship'.*

To the Brigade I would say simply this ' We shall start earning our pay as a team shortly; and we are in this game to win'. "

Captain Peter Jackson. **Southern Evening Echo,** 12th June 1994.

"It's been a most worrying trip for me".

*"The important thing was that we concealed ourselves at all times by our speed, by the route we took and with the assistance of the weather. The **QE2** is so fast that you can disappear. To the best of my knowledge we were only sighted by one ship all the way down on the outward voyage".*

"I have never seen so many icebergs in my life before, I was very thankful for a very fine radar".

Editorial comment. **Daily Mail.** 13th June 1982.

*"Yesterday, at Southampton, Britain's greatest passenger liner, the **QE2**, returned with the survivors and wounded of the Royal Navy ships, **Coventry**, **Antelope** and **Ardent**. The tumultuous welcome of the huge crowd ashore reflected the feelings of gratitude of the whole nation to those who have fought bravely and endured so much for us all.*

The cheers also echoed the universal sense of relief that this great ship, which sailed so swiftly with 3000 troops down to the South Atlantic where it was a prime target for the Argentines, has returned unharmed.

It was a wonderful achievement to take this 67,000 ton vessel with her precious complement of men and material, to keep her out of danger from enemy aircraft and submarines, but in waters thick with icebergs, transfer them to troop carriers and then return with the crews of ships which went down gallantly fighting the enemy.

*We bid both the **QE2** and all those who have returned in her a prosperous voyage into the future".*

From **Air Force Magazine.** December 1982.

*"If the Argentines had received similar intelligence, (American satellite intelligence reported to have been given to the British) they feel certain they would have sunk the **Queen Elizabeth 2,** a prize they badly wanted."*

*"The Argentines did set forth in a Boeing 707 at 18,000 feet one day in search of the **Queen Elizabeth 2"***

QE 2 - "Driving the New Hotel". - 1987

In the almost forgotten days of the steam turbine, slowing down the *QE2* from full sea speed of 29 knots would often cause the First Officer on the bridge some heart stopping moments. Because of the need to reduce speed gradually and therefore allow the turbines to cool evenly (in normal operation!) it was common to allow as much as fifty miles in the last two and a half hours prior to picking up the pilot. This necessitated the Officer of the Watch to constantly monitor the ships position and the rate of reduction in speed, to ensure the ship was at the pilot station with the engines ready to manoeuvre.

Naturally, because the engines were slowed down 'manually' by the engineer on watch, the rate of slowing down often varied depending on who the engineer was. Some of the younger chaps were more 'ambitious' than the experienced hand, which on more than one occasion resulted in the ship being ready to receive the pilot, i.e. at a speed of approximately eight knots, ten miles before the pilot boat! This was of course more acceptable than the other option, which occasionally required the First Officer to make a 'dogs leg', or alternatively to go steaming past the boat, leaving the pilot behind shouting nautically flavoured language over the VHF telephone, and the Captain staring stonily over the bridge wing, no doubt wishing he or preferably his O.O.W. were on leave, or on any other ship but his.

Those days have gone. We now have the largest marine diesel electric plant in the world, with a control system adaptable to even the most unpredictable navigators. Instead of fifty miles in two hours we take about eight miles in the last half an hour and even this is possibly the worst scenario. During our protracted sea trials one of the many manoeuvres we made was the 'crash stop'. This required the stopping distance to be measured from a speed of thirty knots. Not only did the *QE 2* stop in 0.75 of a nautical mile, but in a time of three minutes and forty two seconds, surely a feat to impress even the most sceptical of our critics and one to reassure those of us whose task it is to embark pilots at the right place at the correct time.

This ability to stop easily whenever we wish, without undue stress or fatigue on the machinery, can be mainly attributed to the controllable pitch propellers. Prior to the major refit we had two six bladed propellers, the blades of which were fixed. To go astern the shafts had to be first slowed and then reversed. Now the shafts rotate in one direction all the time, and at a speed of 142 RPM whilst we are 'deep sea', although this is reduced to 70 RPM as we enter pilotage waters. The ships' speed and direction is changed by adjusting the 'angle of attack' of the propeller blades. Instead of the old wheelhouse telegraphs we have 'combinators', two short levers which act very much like an accelerator on a car. Of course the levers are not coupled directly to the engines; there is a very sophisticated 'power management unit' which controls the rate of change of the pitch angle and thus the speed of the ship, particularly at high shaft RPM, so there is still a certain amount of thinking ahead to be done and of course the prudent navigator will always remember that machines are only human! - things can occasionally go wrong.

When we wish to slow down, the combinators, or pitch control levers, are brought slowly back from the full forward position. This changes the pitch angle of the propeller blades and consequently the load to drive the ship at her full sea speed, now approximately 31 knots, which requires all of our 9 diesels to be running and provides electricity to power the large electric motors directly coupled to the propeller shafts. As the load decreases, diesels are shut down automatically but remain available for immediate start up should conditions warrant. During times of 'harbour steaming' the PMU is on 'combinator' mode, which maintains a certain number of diesels on line and gives the pilot almost instantaneous control of the ships speed and direction. In fact the pitch control is capable, when being handled by the more dextrous of navigators, of moving the ship as little as one or two feet up the quay.

Naturally the march of progress dictates the ever increasing use of computers, however, it is reassuring to know that through the initial teething troubles that the QE 2 experienced with her new heart, our friends the engineers were quite capable of stepping in, taking control and sorting out the gremlins which inevitably occur with a sophisticated plant such as ours. From an operational point of view, it is indeed a rare privilege to be given the responsibility of driving what may be the last of the great superliners and the flagship of the British Merchant Navy. May she continue, as the Cunard Line would wish, to sail on and into the twenty first century.

Published in 'Cruise Digest', Vol.6, 1987.

Cunard Princess - "A Week Down Mexico Way"

I'm fairly certain that it was the tourists who were following the whales originally, these days I'm not so sure. The cruise ships start their migration from Alaska by early October and a majority end up on the Mexican run, jockeying for berths and anchorage's wherever they go. The whales reach the fun just before Christmas and what a spectacle it is! Cabo San Lucas, that most southerly tip of Lower California, is a small bay renown on the west coast for its sport fishing, where one ship in the anchorage looks significant, two looks busy and four ridiculous.

Four thousand souls are ejected by tender for four hours on terra firma, giving just enough time for the taxi drivers to use a couple of gallons of petrol in exchange for a couple of months wages, the shopkeepers to lighten their endless load of sombreros - never to be worn again after another week, and the barkeepers to drain yet another vat of tequila, distilled no doubt, next door.

The 813 mile run down from Los Angeles takes just a day and a half, enough time for passengers to find their cabin, the restaurant and the Showboat Lounge, plus of course the outdoor cafe, where that raging hunger that occurs between breakfast, lunch, dinner and the midnight buffet, can be suitably quashed with the ubiquitous burger, hot dog or healthy salad - with plenty of dressing! Scenery is intermittent and dependent on visibility, but the approach to Cabo, with the sandy barren slopes of Cabo Falso, is not dissimilar to an Arabian image. Marine life abounds, dolphins chase the bow wave, whales proceed in their sedentary pace, sighted by their spray and occasionally by their tails reaching out as they dive for deeper water, even seals lie on their backs with their flappers spread wide to take the sun. All this causes feverish activity amongst some, indigestion with others, and judging by what my sailors have to scrub off the decks, at least a few bottles of 'tropical tan' to go flying. But the schedule is relentless - no lazy Sunday ramble this.

Getting 800 passengers ashore and back aboard in four hours using ships launches is not easily achieved. Organisation created by experience creates a thinly disguised disciplined operation - if only the passengers would do what's asked of them. Complaints are regular and expected; everyone wants to step ashore as soon as the anchor touches the bottom. Each launch takes fifty, loading takes ten minutes, the ride in five, unloading another five - simple arithmetic leads to a ready understanding of the logistical problem - unless you've paid $499 for the holiday of a lifetime, are easily misled and, dare I say it, American. I can only assume that people expect that TV series to be 'like it is'!

I often take a launch in, partly to say I've been ashore, but also to have first hand experience of the current problems, satisfy myself the operation is running as smoothly as we can hope for, and watch the folks enjoy their first taste of freedom for almost two days. It's quite surprising how difficult some people find trying to relax, when all the cares and worries are taken away, the little things are magnified to extreme, for example leaving the sunglasses in the cabin drawer can become a major issue between husband and wife, 'Do we have to get another launch ticket if we go back aboard?' or 'Why do we stay such a short time here?', 'What happens if we miss the last launch back?' - for the twenty eighth time. Patience is not a virtue, it is an absolute Godsend.

And then, suddenly it seems, the traffic between the ships thins out, a windlass cranks, chains rumble and crash to a pile in the locker, the anchor emerges, 'sighted and clear' from the fo'c'stle. First the little *Polaris* takes a slow arc close by the rocks and out of the bay, *Bermuda Star* backs out from a gap between *Dawn Princess* and *Cunard Princess* - it seems the Captain with the most nerve, or the most skill, gets the better 'hole' and being first doesn't mean the best position. Just like your local car park, there's always someone who'll get into the spot you thought was too tight, but then necessity is the mother of invention.

193 miles across the Baha to Mazatlan, probably Mexico's biggest port on the Pacific, but today not big enough for all and the *Dawn* finds herself anchoring again - another day of tender operations when all deck work ceases while the ABs' drive the boats. The *Star* takes the remaining cargo berth and we, fortunately turn and 'park' alongside the passenger quay - between the ferry terminal and the oil terminal. I'm happy, reasonable water pressure on the dock and water trucks at $31 each will mean we'll leave full of fresh water tonight - just another of the Mate's worries.

Mazatlan is boat drill day, known to us all as Board of Trade Sports - well at least to that minority on board this Bahamian registered vessel who look back to the days of sailing under the red duster. Still, fun and games and in my exalted status as overlord, I enjoy the developing drama from my vantage point on the boat deck. The Chief Officer's bark is worse than his bite and this is the day it shows; no doubt the effigies and the voodoo will be out in the crew accommodation tonight! The practise however, means that when we do a drill in front of the US Coastguard, they will be suitably impressed. How can it be that with a ship of thirty seven different nationalities we manage to get our act together? I know why.

The other Mates have the bridge visit in the afternoon - if they haven't suffered enough already today. For those who've never seen our office before, it can appear awesome, especially when you explain that there is only one officer on duty at a time, 'Wow!, all these dials and buttons, how do you know which one to press?' - sometimes I ask myself that question.

By six we are ready to sail, with all crew and passengers hopefully on the right ship; 'Senor Frogs' margaritas cause havoc among the unwary, still, all the ships will be in Puerto Vallarta tomorrow. By the time we have crossed another 182 sea miles the *Dawn Princess* has raced ahead, not to be outdone yet again. The *Tropical* however, has taken the only alongside berth, and the *Dawn* anchors, much to our consternation, on the leading marks. There is only one slot left in the tiny harbour, just big enough for our 17,495 tonnes. The Captain deftly manoeuvres our ship round the stern of the *Dawn*, does a 180 degree turn and creeps stern first towards the entrance, meanwhile the pilot, now on his third ship of the morning attempts to anchor the Dawn again. He boards our ship, after the bow has passed the entrance buoys, and too late to be of any real assistance, but his boat will be used to run our stern lines to the shore. As we pass the *Tropical* the stern is swung to port (thank heavens for calm winds and a good bow thruster), until we are parallel. First the port anchor and then the starboard anchor are let go, the fo'c'sle officer jumps from one side to another, two shackles, three, brake open, hold on, anchors in gear, heave on both, tightening the stern lines until the ship is in position a mere 150 feet from that other recent addition to the floating condominium fraternity, - who said seamanship was dead?

0730 Hours, we're in position, moored, the pontoon is down and ready to board our first shore bound revellers. Few takers however, the clocks went forward one hour last night and that innocent enthusiasm has lapsed after only two days - Mexico, been there! But come they eventually do, squinting as they emerge from the shell door into bright sunlight. By this time the 150 foot gap is a mass of boats of all sizes, eager to pick up their organised excursions, deep sea fishing, snorkelling, island tours, booze cruises. The *Star* has arrived and anchored outside and a newcomer to the area, the four masted *Sea Cloud* has dignified the surroundings with her presence; she too has to search the shelf outside for a ledge shallow enough to place her anchor.

By noon the ship is quiet. For a few precious hours we feel just a little relaxed and I take the opportunity to escape. Permission is granted to step back in time, the Bosun runs number seven boat outside the harbour and drops me off at the foot of the Sea *Cloud's* gangway. This prestigious barque built for Marjorie Merriweather Post on her marriage to E.F.Hutton in 1931, had been rescued from dereliction in 1978 by a group of eight German shipowners and industrialists. From lying forlorn in Cristobal, she is today a wonderful example of a ship that is lovingly cared for by everyone who works on board, the varnish work is superb, the brass shining, the wooden decks sea white. Captain Shannon, her unassuming and pleasant American Master was the Master of U.S. Coast Guard sail training ship *Eagle* for ten years. The two hours I spent on board were a porthole into the past which, no doubt, her sixty or so passengers will only appreciate after they return to their busy 20th century lives.

After brief conversations on my hand held VHF, (what did we do before radios?) the Bosun returns in number 7 with a few gallons of black paint, fair payment I think, and I'm speedily removed from the scene. We pick up a few stragglers on the quayside and return to the ship, the boats are hoisted, the pontoon stowed, stations called. The operation of departing is no less fraught as the wind on the beam is now brisk; as soon as the ropes are let go aft, the stern has to be carefully held up with dextrous use of the twin screws while the anchors are heaved home and we power out of the harbour, three long blasts as we go.

The return voyage commences, and the passengers try to take advantage of the sun to finish off that tan, but it quickly gets cooler. A deep low has passed over Los Angeles and we're feeling the effects already. The following morning we pass close to Cabo yet again, *Stardancer and Pacific Princess* are making their four hour call, they too will soon be following us north. 1700 hours Thursday and we are passing the island of Santa Margarita, the late afternoon gives a golden hue to the hills which rise 1800 feet from the rocky barren foreshore. The lighthouse on Cape San Lazaro looks like some long forgotten fort from 'Beau Geste'.

As we emerge from the lee of Cerros Island on Friday morning, the weather deteriorates even further, we're pitching now and spray is passing level with the bridge wings. This is not usual around here at this time of year. A north westerly wind, force 5, plus the ships speed of 17 knots can cause a certain amount of 'mal de mer' - not the best of endings for a holiday. Fortuitously we have some speed in hand and can afford to come down to three engines, 14.5 knots, in the late afternoon, consequently the motion eases - too late for some.

Night arrives and with it sleep, tomorrow is another day, another cruise. Our cargo walks off a little browner, a little heavier and a little poorer. For us life continues with our very own version of 'the daily grind', our grass though, is certainly greener on this side of the hill.

10th. March 1989.

Published in "Ships Monthly" November 1989

Scandinavian Saga - First Command.

During the early part of 1990 I was offered the position of Master with a Florida based company whose vessels specialised in the one day cruise market. The decision to leave Cunard, where I had been employed for twelve years and had risen to the position of Chief Officer, was not an easy one. I realised that another ten years could pass before I might attain that most honourable of maritime positions if I were to stay, a prospect I found both daunting and depressing. The cruise industry although expanding overall, was stagnant with respect to British officers being employed on British ships.

I left England at the end of August, spending a day in Miami visiting the head office of 'SeaEscape' and suffering the inevitable medical. Within a week I had sailed for a few days on the Scandinavian Sun, had a day on board the *Scandinavian Dawn* (ex Sealink *St.George*) which was completing a refit in Freeport, Bahamas and finally joined the *Scandinavian Saga* for familiarisation and ship handling experience.

The company had at that time three vessels operating one day cruises out of Port Everglades, Miami and St.Petersburg, Florida. The *Dawn* was converting and two more ships were in the pipe line. With this amount of activity, manning arrangements needed to be somewhat flexible, consequently I never returned to the *Dawn* where I had expected to relieve the Master for his vacation. After a few days on the *Saga* I took over the Staff captains position to learn the new role in which I found myself - for better or for worse! The duties were much the same as those of Chief Officer on my

The "*Worcester*" – 1969
– Where it all started

"Gallic Minch"
1976

"Gallic Minch"
– The distinctive bow

"*QEII*" at anchor, Grytviken 1982

Troops on departure   Taking on supplies off Ascension

Inhospitable Grytviken, South Georgia

Chartroom "*Reina Del Mar*" 1973

"*Reina Del Mar*"
In South America
1973

In the cockpit of the SRN4 Hovercraft 1978

Publicity shot for Cunard Line 1979

Being introduced to
The Queen Mother
1982

Crew photo "*Fantasy World*" 1993

"*The Empress*" 1994

"Bayleaf"; refuelling *"QEII"* at sea

Navigator at work

"Pride of San Diego", ex-*"Scandinavian Saga"* 1990

Preparing to sail from
St Petersburg.
"Scandinavian Song"
future *"The Empress"*
in the background
1990.

The murder ship "*Coral Princess*" 1993

"*Fantasy World*" 1993

Bow damage to "*The Empress*" 1994

In the Singapore repair yard

previous ships. Captain Glan Phillips, an expatriate Welshman, took me under his wing and had to suffer the heart stopping surges of adrenaline which any Master has to deal with when handing over the controls of his only source of income to a perfect stranger.

I look back with sincere gratitude for those few weeks of initial training. Initially my dockings were traumatic but relatively controlled, however, for no apparent reason the ship would, at times, do quite the opposite of what might be expected, my confidence would rise, only to be shattered a few days later. Double rings astern on both engine room telegraphs were not unknown. Just one day before I was due to take over command, a close call with the dock was just avoided by Glan's appreciation of the situation. I learnt that 'small speeds means small dents' and to 'always have room to make one more ahead movement with the engines'. Sound advice.

The *Scandinavian Saga* had been built in Greece in 1974 as the *Castalia* for Hellenic Mediterranean Lines. Gross tonnage was 7,768, length 433 feet, twin screws and a bow thruster, originally operating as a car ferry between Italy and Greece. Unlike my previous vessels she was not fitted with bridge control or controllable pitch propellers. When docking the ship the Master shouts his engine orders into the wheelhouse from the wings, the steering and thruster being controlled from outside. A somewhat disjointed way of putting a ship alongside the dock - imagine trying to park your car with the passenger operating the foot pedals!

At that time the ship was operating four days a week to Freeport from Miami and three days to the island of Bimini where she would anchor, the passengers being ferried ashore for a two hour 'beach bash'. Weather had been excellent, calm seas and temperatures in the 90's. Winter was approaching however and on October 9th, my first day in command, it arrived!

We left on schedule a little after 8:30 am and set off across the Florida Straights, where the warm ocean current of the Gulf Stream flows north at three or four knots. A cold front was approaching and the wind was gusting up to force seven, the net affect being a short steep sea and swell reaching fifteen feet which, needless to say, was causing a certain amount of discomfort among the passengers. The average 'day cruiser', if there is such an animal, is not known for his ability to retain the contents of his stomach, much of which was hastily transferred to that necessity of sea travel, the 'barf bag' - a quaint American expression unfamiliar to me before this time.

Our speed was reduced from sixteen knots to thirteen as a result of the head seas and high exhaust temperatures on the main engines. Wind gusts of over sixty knots were showing on the anemometer, consequently our arrival at the Freeport pilot station was delayed by over an hour. The pilots were concerned about the weather and recommended two tugs, a suggestion to which I of course prudently agreed. The wind however reduced in strength to twenty knots and berthing was not the problem we had anticipated, the tugs in fact being more of a hindrance with their heavy towing wires. After only a few short hours we departed, without mishap or assistance. It is always much easier to take off than to land!

The return voyage was not the 'event' of the morning, seas had moderated and winds were following. I remember that the boarding of the pilot off Miami was decidedly dangerous, for him not for us, and from my diary I read the docking was 'interesting but satisfactory' - an understatement I'm sure. Strong winds onto the dock can result in difficulty in keeping the ship from landing heavily. The *Saga* has, I discovered, limits of about twenty knots of crosswind to successfully dock without the assistance of a tug.

The bad weather continued for a few more days, emanating from tropical storm 'Marco' which passed to the south of Florida and into the Gulf of Mexico. Our next two trips to Bimini were cancelled, there being insufficient sheltered water off the island. With the wind blowing from any direction other than east, launch operations could be hazardous, even the slightest swell resulted in horrifying gaps between ship and tender, punctuated by frightening crunching noises as the two vessels came back together, bending the railings, buckling gangways and scaring old ladies.

The company were going through a rescheduling phase. I was instructed to leave Miami on Saturday morning at 4 a.m. and take the vessel to

St.Petersburg in Tampa Bay. Consequently, Friday 12th. saw us take one last trip across the Straits to Bimini, returning to Miami for two hours, sail again with a thousand passengers on a 'party cruise', returning at 3 a.m. At 4:25 I sailed again, an engine problem causing the slight delay. No doubt some mariners would consider the one day cruise market the 'soft option' or an easy way of going to sea, but I believe the schedule speaks for itself.

The four hundred mile journey around the southern tip of Florida took just over twenty hours. I picked the pilot up at 6 a.m. on Sunday and arrived alongside at 9. Over three hundred passengers were waiting to embark and we sailed again at 10 a.m. on a cruise to 'nowhere', returning at 8:30 p.m. There was barely sufficient time to take water and fuel bunkers for the next voyage, a three day cruise to Mexico - we left at midnight.

My first undocking at St.Petersburg turned out to be yet another event. The pilot, who had the unfortunate name of Cropper, was quite happy for me to back the ship around out of the relatively small basin and into the channel. As we came off the berth we lost the port engine, I continued manoeuvring on one engine and the bow thruster but found I was turning to short. It was then that the Chief Engineer phoned and said he had lost most of the engine starting air. Again, imagine yourself trying to remove your car from a parking space when some misguided fool has hemmed you in during your absence - a little difficult when the wheels will only turn in one direction. I was informed we had just one engine start left, and I'm backing myself into an even smaller hole. Not to be outdone, I used the one start to stop any further astern movement, but by now the ship is moving ahead with insufficient room to swing the bow or the stern!

It is perhaps at times like this when all the experience in the world tells you that you are not going to get away without mishap, and a certain resignation starts to set in. Yet I find that my seemingly endless years of training and watching stimulates, not panic, but a quiet determination to persevere. I tried to get one more engine start, got it, then dropped the port anchor - the ship swung gradually out of the hole of my own making. For all the dockings I've watched other Masters make, there is no substitute to doing the job yourself, have things go wrong and getting out of the situation using your own skill and experience. It isn't really scientific, it's certainly not computerised, it's just using what you've got to your advantage, the machinery, the elements and in the early stages almost the 'seat of your pants'!

The cruise to Cozumel in Mexico is used primarily for the purpose of revalidating the United States visas of the foreign crew on board the vessel. The ship has to go 'foreign' once a month to satisfy a quirk of the U.S. Immigration Service, but the trip is a pleasant interlude from the daily routine and with cabins for just over three hundred passengers, the ship is like a small select club for a very few days. The usual ship board activities prevail and I even host a Captains Cocktail Party, not quite so dressy as my Cunard days, but entertaining none the less. A friendly atmosphere, enlivened this particular trip by a large group of Savannah Georgia 'Shaggers' who all but took over. The 'shag' I am reliably informed is a particular style of American country dancing.

Three days soon pass, Cozumel for eight hours is just an interlude and we soon return to our daily schedule, 10 a.m. departure, 8:30 p.m. return, with two cruises on Friday and Saturday when we finally dock at 2:30 in the morning. A certain degree of tedium can set in if not fought off with enthusiasm and the satisfaction of seeing the schedule maintained, and the appearance of the ship both inside and out kept up to the standards one might expect. Inspection of crew quarters, galleys, storerooms, etc., are carried out routinely, safety drills come around like clockwork and every three months they are witnessed by the United States Coastguard who verify that our weekly drills and procedures are up to internationally recognised standards. Perhaps most importantly the staff are encouraged in their work, a smile and a 'good morning' from the Captain goes a long way I find.

The short cruise 'experience' must be one of activity, friendliness and informality. There must be good entertainment, good food and good service, but most of all their must be that quantity which the first time cruiser expects, but is unknown and not realised till the voyage is over and looked back upon respectively. The customers are the best advertisement and the best hope for future business.

To comply with the local regulations we had to travel 'three leagues' from the mainland before we could open the ship's casino, which is of course a big money earner on board a one day ship. Gambling, which includes slot machines, is allowed in only a very few places in the USA, Las Vegas and Atlantic City being examples. To reach the required distance meant a thirty five mile journey around Tampa Bay, which necessitated our taking a local pilot who would stay on board all day, resting for the few hours the ship was anchored outside territorial waters.

Some of these seamen were characters, Walter Egan, seventy two years old, remembered going to sea on the *Leviathan*. He told me many stories in the hours we spent on the bridge together. An expatriate Australian called Cahill, or the 'Roo', was engaged to a female Second Mate from an American tanker, he drank lager and tomato juice mixed! There was an ex tug skipper from Texas who spoke in a Southern drawl and regularly lost more money in the casino than his daily earnings would be, and Fred Smith who invariably brought a box of doughnuts to keep the bridge team happy. All interesting and individual men who had served their time at sea and opted for the satisfying work of driving ships every day but spending life always close to home.

In seven weeks we carried close to twenty two thousand passengers and I made one hundred and seventy dockings/undockings, happily without mishap. There were some of course that were more difficult than others and I also found the problems of training someone else. I allowed the Staff Captain to manoeuvre the ship on several occasions when I believed the conditions to be suitable. I found myself reflexing much the same way as a husband does when he teaches his wife to drive! There is a fine line when judging where to step in and correct a developing situation and at the same time trying to avoid destroying the confidence of the trainee, one discovers yet another facet of one's character.

In early December we sailed away from the Bay and made for Mobile, Alabama to complete the bottom and annual surveys required by the Classification Society, along with other maintenance work which could not be carried out afloat or with the ship in service. Another of the company vessels had taken over the St.Petersburg service and my ship was bound eventually for California, a charterer intended starting a new service from San Diego to Ensenada in Mexico. I took a short vacation, rejoining the ship a few days before the inaugural voyage.

I was to complete another three months with *Scandinavian Saga,* but with her new name *Pride of San Diego.* The charter was unfortunately not a success, one of the reasons being strong competition from a Greek shipowner who had managed to start a service a few weeks before. The charterer lost money, ceased trading and SeaEscape was left with a ship on their hands just at the time they were also in financial difficulty. I could see the writing on the wall and during my next leave I managed to secure another Master's position out in the Far East. My first command had been an interesting period; professionally I had become a ship handler as well as a Master, it was to be the start of a new phase in my life.

Sembawang Johnson Management 1991.

Cora Princess.

During March 1991 I was offered command of the *Cora Princess.* This old lady, built in 1963 as *Princesa Leopoldina,* was best known as Swires *Coral Princess*, operating cruises in the Far East for many years until being sold to Hong Kong owners Universal Boss in late 1990.

I wasn't quite sure what to expect, the ship being managed by a Singapore Company but on charter to Indonesian interests. Effectively I could have been working for three groups. I was unaware of it's trading activity other than it was on a four day round trip, Singapore to Jakarta, which didn't sound to unpleasant.

My initial flight was cancelled as a result of bad weather, consequently I arrived in Singapore on the morning of May 22nd., had a brief interview with the Operations Manager Mr.James Seah and the Managing Director Mr.Lars Sjogren, then down to the ship which had arrived that morning at berth M 19, a cargo wharf near the container terminal. Fortunately I was to sail for a round voyage with the incumbent Master, another Englishman, Captain Andrew Wilson, who was to explain the rudiments of the business. Apparently, although there was a cruise aspect, the main revenue was generated in the casino and in fact the operation was financially the biggest floating casino world-wide.

I took a few days to familiarise myself with the ship and staff. There was nothing complicated or strenuous about the run, departing from the two ports around 1800 hours and arriving, after a day and two nights at sea, at 0830 hours. The route followed was via Banka Straight, thus giving calm waters for most of the voyage, these waters being sheltered from the prevailing monsoon. This was in fact very necessary as our mainly Indonesian Chinese 'clientele' were very susceptible to the slightest motion and the casino, which was open all the time the vessel was in international waters, would abruptly clear if the ship started to roll.

The ship was rather cumbersome to manoeuvre having twin screws but only one rudder and no bow thruster, consequently two tugs were usually taken during berthing operations. In the port of Singapore the pilots and tugs are generally very good, the pilots hopping from one ship to another in a port where I was told there are over 7000 piloted movements a month. The port of Jakarta is Tanjung Priok and here it is sometimes difficult to understand the way the pilot's mind is working, similarly, the tugs do not appear to be on a similar wavelength. English is not widely spoken or understood so that the operation of docking is often carried out with nods and grunts of semi - understanding. Having said that, I was fortunate and there was never any mishap or accident. Delays were of course inevitable, both to arriving and leaving, but as our schedule was unhurried, it never seemed to matter!

During the holiday periods of Singapore we may have carried up to a hundred Singaporeans who either sailed out and returned home by air after a few days in Indonesia, or made the round trip on the vessel. The players in the casino however, usually only travelled for two days, sometimes flying back to Jakarta only to rejoin a few days later. They were known as Junket, and those designated to organise them were the Junket Leaders. I use the term organise loosely, as most of the time there seemed to be little organisation. In the so called passenger terminal in Tanjung Priok the boarding arrangements appeared chaotic and I was told money often changed hands for one favour or another. The Junket themselves would sit in little groups while their Leaders scurried about the place with handfuls of passports, getting stamps for this and paying a tax for that; most confusing.

I don't recall ever sailing on time, we usually had to wait for one or two VIPs' - big players - who of course had their entourage. I was also informed that the Junket didn't actually pay for their cabins, but guaranteed to deposit up to $10,000 US at the casino cashiers desk, which was in turn exchanged for non redeemable chips - in other words they had to be played and if the player won he would be given chips he could then cash. Hundreds of thousands of dollars could be won or lost during a two day voyage.

I remained with the ship for three months during which time the Charterers started becoming increasingly careful about their expenditure. They had no previous experience of operating a large passenger vessel nor were they aware of the expenses involved. Before I left the, Charterers representatives took over the purchasing of all food stores and at one stage appeared on the ship with Indonesian food previously cooked ashore, put into plastic dustbins and was telling our chef he would only have to reheat before serving! I would not accept it - my years of experience with US port health regulations told me to be sceptical of cost savings made this way and the possible health complications that could arise as a result. I don't think the authorities would be too impressed if I took a ship into their port with two or three hundred cases of gastro enteritis on board

On the 29th of June I had possibly my saddest and hardest decision to make. Sometime during the previous night, crew member Hla U Min, a Burmese utility hand, jumped overboard. He had only been with the ship a few weeks and during the ensuing investigation I discovered he had been unhappy and possibly of unsound mind. His absence was reported to me after breakfast and a search of the ship revealed no presence of his whereabouts. It seems he must have left his cabin in the very early hours and not returned. The ship would have been following the channels off Sinkep Island in the Berhala Straight and by the morning we were some considerable distance ahead. I had an urgency message passed to the local authorities and advised all vessels in the area to keep a sharp lookout, but I decided against turning around because I considered the time involved and the uncertainty of the hour he went overboard would make the chances of finding him most unlikely.

He was, to my knowledge, never found and the tragic consequences, not only to himself, but to the family who loved him and needed his support, will always be somewhere in the back of my memory. It only takes a look at a mans meagre remaining possessions to put a scar into your own optimistic belief that all's well that ends well.

Orient Sun

The previous Master returned in mid August and I took my vacation back home in the UK, eventually being recalled by Sembawang Johnson to join the *Orient Sun*. She was previously the *Orient Express/Eurosun* and originally the *Bore Star,* a Baltic ferry built in 1975. Her more recent career had been as a cruising vessel for Sea Containers in the Mediterranean. The charterers were the same as for *Cora Princess* and this was when my troubles were about to begin in earnest.

After a brief few days handover I took command on November 13th. That very day I had to delay sailing from Singapore as no machinery lubricating oil had been delivered. The Charterers had taken over the technical purchasing but had no idea how to go about it. Because they had no credit facility large bags of money had to be taken to buy such things as fuel supplies!

The new cruise liner terminal in Singapore had just been opened and we were one of the first ships to use it. Three berths connected to the World Trade Center, a large complex of shops and offices, and far more interesting than the old cargo berth we had previously been allocated. The berth we were to use most regularly was designated CC3, an as yet unfinished dock alongside what was going to be a large exhibition hall.

The new berth proved to cause some interesting manoeuvres for me and fortunately *Orient Sun* had twin controllable pitch propellers, twin rudders and a powerful bow thruster. With 24,000 ships horse power I could almost make the ship walk sideways. The berth was tucked into a corner and the 'T' pier, with CC1 and CC2 on the inside, had to be passed to get into it. If there was a ship on CC1 there was little room left for error and with a strong flood tide setting you down, some interesting moments were had! One particular occasion comes to mind when I decided to let the pilot berth the ship, as the bow thruster was not available. He over compensated when the flood set the bow down and then the tug aft applied too much weight to his line which broke under the strain. I had to use plenty of 'screwing' action to swing the stern away from the *Royal Odyssey*, then more power to prevent the ship coming up against the end of the basin. I found the pilots to be very competent provided they had tugs fast at either end.

At first I used to turn the ship before the Cruise Center and back down into CC3, but the Harbour Authorities accused the vessel of causing disturbance to their new breakwater foundations with the propeller wash, so a forward berthing was required. I preferred on occasion going stern first into a berth as there is always more power available from the engines to push you out of trouble if required, or the rudder to swing the stern away from danger.

We shuttled back and forth to Jakarta every four days and there always seemed to be some problem with the charterers, invariably as a result of non delivery of stores or fuel. Berthing in Tanjung Priok was more acceptable as we didn't require tugs and the pilots just stood and watched, telling me when the ship was finally in position alongside, by which time I already knew anyway. Leaving was even easier, several times the pilot boarded, had his paper signed and left before the ship had moved off the berth. Of course we never sailed on time but the ship had plenty of speed in reserve so we were never late at the other end .

On one occasion in Singapore the Charterers representative, Madame Koo, and her side kick, Serena Yeo, came aboard just over an hour before the scheduled sailing time and told me not to sail as the casino concession had not paid them. This was, I thought, a turn up for the books as I knew the concession 'Ace Casindo' had in fact been supplying cash direct to keep the ship going. It was all political of course, but I refused to take any notice of these two 'clowns' until I had received formal instructions from the Charterer in writing. A flurry of activity occurred with Madame Koo using her two portable phones to talk to Jakarta and Hong Kong simultaneously. One was thrust into my face but I just reiterated my decision. Being a Sunday no one was at our office so I phoned the Managing Director at home. He duly appeared some thirty minutes later still in his sailing gear and looking most irate.

He slammed his fist on the table and repeated my instructions. By this time the passengers had boarded and a port regulation required us to leave the berth by 1830 hours, it being not ready for night time operation. A fax came at 1825 hours authorising me to remain alongside and put the passengers ashore, but sufficient time was no longer available for the passengers to disembark and I took the ship to the anchorage. There was much rumour and speculation on board as we lay there, but around 2130 I received another fax instructing me to sail for Jakarta - and that was the last I heard of that little escapade. It was, however, just a taste of what was to come.

The entertainment on board was superior to *Cora Princess,* but in the main consisted of Chinese acts who would come on for one or two trips. The Cruise Director, Morgan Kent, stayed for a few weeks but was offered I presume a more lucrative position working on board the *Royal Pacific,* a Greek ship which had been chartered by Ace Casino for the same run and which was to sink in August 1992 after being in collision with a Taiwanese fishing boat. I was sorry to lose Morgan as he was an excellent ship's entertainer.

The Yugoslav Chief Engineer, Nick, went home to an embattled Croatia and was replaced by a Swede, 'Pe Pe', who along with his Staff Chief Kristian, proved to be invaluable for their technical ability and for keeping me informed of their own troubles down below.

Things became gradually worse with regard to technical spares and I faxed a letter to the Charterers stressing the need for them to re-stock the vessel as per the charter agreement. Eventually we had to stop one of the four main Pielstick engines as there were no spare exhaust gas valves with which to replace the ones which had burnt out. I sent another fax.

As we arrived back in Singapore on December 20th., a turbo charger blew on another engine, so I was down to one engine on each shaft, with suspect exhaust gas valves on the other two. I therefore decided that I should refuse to sail the vessel that evening as I believed it both unsafe and unwise. I faxed the Charterers again.

My Managing Director was delighted, Madame Koo was not. She arrived down with her entourage of lawyers and technical experts to whom I thrust a bookful of unfulfilled technical stores orders covering the previous three months. They looked down and I knew they agreed with me. Hasty measures were made to deliver the necessary parts. In the meantime, I took the ship out to anchor and also informed the Classification Society and the Singapore Marine Department with whom the ship was registered and I'm pleased to say they both supported my actions and gave preconditions before the ship would be allowed to sail.

The ship remained in Singapores' Western Anchorage overnight, but the following morning, December 21st., I was given instruction to proceed to Singapore's Eastern Working Anchorage where we were to remain until the early hours of the 24th., by which time all four main engines were in good working order and one or two other items had been rectified to my satisfaction. The Charterers were furious but there was nothing they could do. I found out where the 'buck stops' - at my door!

The whole business had of course left a bad taste in my mouth; the Charterers through either ignorance or pure conniving had pushed just a little too far. I heard later from my MD that their first reaction was to 'sack the Captain'.

We continued in service over the Christmas period with no further mention of this last episode, but gradually, over the 'galley radio', I heard reports that the casino concession were intending to pull out. This rumour became very strong by January 6th and on arrival Singapore the following morning I discovered that Ace Casindo intended removing all their machines, tables and associated equipment. The Charterers told us nothing.

The casino was stripped, even down to the lights above the gaming tables, their staff left with their belongings not really knowing where they were to end up. Fuel for the next voyage was not delivered and therefore, as I had not been informed the voyage was to be cancelled, I faxed the Charterers representative a message advising her I could not sail without fuel. The whole business was a political game between the casino concession and the Charterers - we were in the middle.

The following morning I took the vessel out to the anchorage and I heard from my Management around eleven o'clock that the Charterers had cancelled the Charter and that the future employment of the vessel was now uncertain. I presumed it would be for the courts to decide on compensation to the owner.

Over the next week, many of the ship's crew were repatriated which was extreme bad luck as they relied on their ten months contract and meagre wages to support their families in the Philippines, Burma, Malaysia the other Eastern countries from which they came and where good work is hard to find.

The intention of the Management Company was to transfer me to the *Shangri-La-World* when Captain Larsen returned from his vacation on January 23rd. This was the second time he had relieved me on a vessel where the Charter had turned bad. I left the ship on the 24th, still at anchor in the Eastern, where she was to stay for another month before being repositioned to the Baltic and new owners. The spell in the anchorage had been not without incident as we had a fire one night in a passenger cabin, apparently caused by a smouldering cigarette carelessly left by a person unknown. Fortunately the problem was dealt with quickly but there was damage to the area and the officer who should have been on the bridge was dismissed for being absent and thus not being aware of the automatic fire alarm.

Shangri-La-World / Asean World.

On the 27th of January I joined *Shangri-La-World,* the ex-Norwegian Cruise Lines *Skyward,* which was working for different Charterers but on a similar trade. Originally intended for the Jakarta Singapore run, there had been many problems from the start when the Authorities in Jakarta had refused the entry permission after an alleged gambling rule infraction. In fact it had again been a political nonsense between different groups and it seemed ours didn't have as much 'clout' as the other - or at least were not prepared to pay as much 'back hand' money as was expected. Great efforts were made to have the ban lifted, even to changing the ships name to *Asean World*. Nothing worked so we continued on four day round trip voyages to Phuket, Thailand's holiday island on the west coast. The island is very pleasant and was to give much pleasure to the crew. The berth was originally built for the export of tin and although not big, was of ample size for our vessel. The weather was fine and I rarely used a tug. The pilot boarded on arrival but always watched the departure from the quayside - most civilised.

Asean World, named after the five countries of the Association of South Eastern Nations, was more of a luxury vessel compared to both *Cora Princess* and *Orient Sun,* and the service on board tried to reflect that. I was to stay two months and in that time we had none of the problems previously experienced. Many of the regular 'players' would fly from Jakarta to Singapore to take the vessel and one in particular I remember, referred to only as Mr. Wong, came about every eight days and usually left in Phuket two million dollars lighter! One of the Charterers, Mr. La Tief, would sail with him and several times I was asked to expedite the docking to ensure this little ensemble reached the airport in time to catch their flights. This proved interesting on one occasion when the port engine was not available for docking (due to a turbo charger failure; fortunately the weather was fair, the tug was available and I had become sufficiently confident not to be too worried.

I left the ship after being out of the UK for four months and went up to Trinity House in London to sit the examination for Deep Sea Pilot, after which I was fortunate enough to work for the Hutchinson agency. I was not to return to the Far East for almost a year, when I was yet again to join *Asean World* by which time it had been renamed yet again - *Fantasy World,* her third change but not the last as I was also to be aboard her as *Continental World* and *Leisure World*. Only the Charterers, who also changed, really knew the reason behind all the different names; certainly the ship must hold the record for so many names in such a relatively short interval of time.

North Sea Pilotage.

I had for some time considered taking the license to become a Deep Sea Pilot. These men board ships to take them up the English Channel and on to the North Sea ports of the United Kingdom and the rest of Europe, offering inexperienced or overworked Masters the benefit of a competent licensed seaman to assist with the navigation in the sometimes hazardous waters around our coasts.

The Corporation of Trinity House is the body delegated by our Government to examine and license deep sea pilots. In London their headquarters are at Tower Hill in an imposing building opposite the Tower of London and it was to here that I ventured in the early part of 1992 with the intention of obtaining this most respected of nautical qualifications.

I had studied the charts and prepared a bridge book for one of the 'Elder Brothers' to inspect and I expected a tough time during the examination, which is an oral one only, as I had not actually been up the Channel for five years, the last time being on the *QE 2*. Only officers who have been Master for at least one years sea time may apply for the examination and it is necessary for you to prove you can safely navigate any vessel through the channel at any time.

The examination in fact was not particularly difficult, even though the conference table had been set out with many charts, Admiralty Pilots, tide tables, etc. For sure I did not know all the courses and distances around the channel in my head, but I had most of them down in my bridge book, a large tome of information gathered in an A4 loose leaf file. I proved my courses by taking out my own charts and obviously satisfied the Elder Brother as to my knowledge, and he issued me initially with a limited draught license. I had to carry out six pilotage acts with vessels below thirty eight foot draught before I could be let loose on the largest super tanker.

I was never to reach anywhere near that draught during my piloting time, but I was lucky enough to be taken on by Deep Sea and Coastal Pilots as soon as I let the elderly Captain Hutchinson know I had a license. Within a few days he sent me off to join the Indian cargo vessel *State of Orissa,* and what a state it was. Boarding off Brixham by pilot boat, I climbed the ladder and was introduced to the Master and shown my cabin, a small drab room with no carpet and only painted bulkheads to look at, the small shower room looked decidedly seedy and I was later to learn that the toilet did not flush (bucket handily provided) and the shower only ran cold.

The run up to Antwerp was routine and completed in reasonable weather. Apart from stopping the Chief Officer from going the wrong side of a buoy, my services were hardly required. After arrival I had to prepare my self for the return voyage and to keep myself occupied during the interval, and so, as with all my pilotage trips, it was this interval of waiting that was the most frustrating - a good book is only part of the answer to alleviating the boredom. After what seemed an interminable time, but was only about four days, the ship left and sailed over to Teesport where I was glad to depart and take the long train ride down to my home in Cornwall.

Over the next ten months I was to pilot 11 different vessels, some more than once. The *Green Ridge* was an American cargo vessel of 9,514 tonnes on charter to the US Defence Department. Her cargo was ammunition and I actually went aboard three times, always going up to Nordenham on the German Weser river. The permanent Master was a man in his forties but still with an appearance one could associate with a sixties hippie, long thinning hair in a pony tail and a long beard. A relaxed atmosphere on board made the first trip interesting and there seemed to be little concern about the nature of their cargo.

The second trip I made on the ship was rather protracted as I remained on board during their stay in Germany. I had been without work for a while and as I was only paid for the jobs I did, money was becoming rather short so I needed the trip back down the channel to Brixham which was worth over 450 Pounds. I must have watched most of their videos during my stay in Germany and life was a little dull. The relief Master was a rather overweight man in his early thirties, somewhat nervous with his first command. The ship discharged some ammunition and then commenced loading everything from shells to missiles which I presume had reached their shelf expiry date and had to be returned to the States for reprocessing. There were the usual delays, but finally the last of the cargo, which was in containers, was placed on deck and off we went down the river.

The weather deteriorated as we passed through the North Sea and down into the English Channel, until as we were passing the Kent coast visibility was down to a mile and there was a fair amount of traffic. An RAF Sea King helicopter from the Manston base could be seen flying around conducting exercises; it came quite close and hovered alongside a few hundred yards off. The side door opened and the winchman gesticulated to us as we stared from the bridge wing, I went inside and the pilot was calling us up on the radio. I believed he was just letting us know that he was conducting exercises and I said fine. It had been difficult to hear exactly what he said as the noise from the machine was very loud. The Captain, showing signs of nervousness, said that he hoped the helicopter would come no closer. I reassured him, but then realised that indeed, not only was he coming closer, but he was lowering the winch wire with a man attached down onto the after deck - the old man almost had a fit.

The Captain went off the bridge to meet the intrepid aviator, but he must have gone one way while the airman came up the inside and I was greeted with a big smile as he no doubt thought I was the Captain. He quickly explained the purpose of the exercise and suggested that he be winched off the fordeck. Needless to say I explained the Captain's concern and that a hovering helicopter above a ship full of explosives was perhaps not such a good idea. At that the Captain came back in through the bridge door looking as though he was about to explode! I quickly explained the situation and sent the RAF chap on his way.

114

The situation soon calmed down and the helicopter went off to play on the next ship following us down the Channel. The Captain slowly regained his composure and my embarrassment soon disappeared, but I was quite pleased to take to the pilot ladder later in the day off Brixham.

Amongst the vessels I piloted there were car carriers, refrigerated cargo ships (reefers), and one tanker carrying phosphoric acid, the *Sabarimala,* an Indian vessel of 21,035 gross tonnes. This last vessel I took from Brixham to Rotterdam and back in late November, early December. The weather was reasonable on the way up and as the ship was only six months old I expected few problems. The discharge of the cargo went quick enough and we were soon back on the way south west, crossing the traffic lanes to pass down the English side of the Channel. The sea conditions were picking up with a strong wind blowing from the south west as we cleared Dover and I, having completed over eleven hours on the bridge, went off to put my head down for a few hours. I woke up before midday, took a shower, and was getting dressed when the young Indian third mate came knocking on my door with a request to come onto the bridge as soon as possible. I found the Master somewhat excited and he told me that the port anchor had run out on its own and we were now anchored some twenty miles of Portsmouth.

Apparently the ship had been slamming into the head seas and the windlass brake must have been sufficiently loose to allow a little movement of the anchor; this had become worse until the brake held no longer - and down it went! Fortunately the old man had the presence of mind to pull back on the engine control and the ship was stopped before all the cable could be dragged out of the chain locker. Even so the depth of water was well over twenty meters and most of the cable was outside the ship. The master asked me to stay on the bridge while he went off with the Mate to the fo'c'stle to see what could be done to retrieve the errant chain.

Unfortunately something mechanical had become bent or broken inside the windlass and even though I was taking the weight off the chain by using the engine, it could not be hoisted. We went on for about four hours like this until finally a very large hammer was found and, in true heavy engineering style, a few well directed blows solved the problem and the chain was returned to the locker. The light was just going so it was fortuitous that they succeeded when they did, even so it meant a late arrival for me off Brixham and I was to miss the last train of the day back to Cornwall.

I never really had very bad weather when I was piloting, even so there were a few uncomfortable moments boarding and disembarking from ships, and having to climb the ladder up or down onto the pilot boat which may be riding the seas some way below the deck. The secret to disembarking in bad weather was to make sure you gave the boat a good lee, in other words to place the ship in such a position that it sheltered the pilot boat if only for a few minutes. Of course this was not always easy to do in rough weather. If you slowed down too soon or turned too early the ship would start to roll leaving the pilot boat to rise and fall perhaps more than twenty feet by the time it was alongside. Judging the speed just right it was possible to get close up to the land, swing the ship towards its new course, call the pilot boat in and take a run down through the accommodation, onto the deck and down the ladder waving a glad good-bye to the luckless Captain and his crew who had to press on into no doubt increasing seas of the Western Approaches.

The large car carriers were the most awkward ships to handle, but fortunately in the main I had plenty of sea room in which to carry out my manoeuvres. I actually piloted five of them and the Japanese owned *Fuji* was my last ship. By the end of 1992 I had had so few ships that I was becoming a little desperate. I was the extra man and not on the divided 'pool' money of the other regular pilots, only being paid for the ships I worked, and then the agent took 15% which left me with not a lot if I'd only been away for a few days.

I anticipated having to work over Christmas, and needless to say, I received a call to join the 47,751 gross tonne *Fuji* in Avonmouth on December 23rd. The ship was on charter to NYK line and was bringing vehicles in from Japan. The Captain and Chief Engineer were Japanese, just about all the other crew were Filipino and when I boarded I realised that my Christmas was going to be non existent.

116

From Avonmouth we sailed to Cherbourg, Antwerp, Sheerness, Rotterdam, Bremerhaven, Zeebruge, Southampton, Le Havre and finally back past Brixham where I disembarked on January 5th. Not only was it the busiest pilotage trip I had encountered, but also the longest. We just about missed any port delay because of public holidays as we were at sea on Christmas day and New Years day. There were no celebrations on board, in fact because of the hectic schedule there was really no time to celebrate, but I think perhaps after I left them the crew would have been able to relax a little. The Captain looked exhausted by the time I left, even though I had hardly seen him on the bridge during the sea passages and it was a good example of the reason for ensuring sea pilots are available, to help overworked Master's with third world crews on these very tiring coastal passages.

The *Fuji* was my last ship as a sea pilot, I had not had sufficient work to keep our bank balance in the black and Sembawang Johnson wanted me back out in Singapore. It was a bitter blow to our family who had, in the early part of the year, thought that I would be based at home for good and the long periods of enforced absence were over. Over the next few years I kept my license valid by returning to Trinity House every January, being interviewed and paying my 100 pounds. There was still no offer of a place on the pool; Hutchinson retired and the company who took over appeared to lose some of their regular business. Hammonds in Dover, the other deep sea pilotage agency, kept my name on file, but it seemed the shipping business was again in recession and one of the first things companies could drop was non compulsory pilotage. When eventually Hammonds phoned in early '96 suggesting a place may be available in April, I asked what the average pilots wage had been for the previous year; it had been not much more than half of the salary I had received as Master on the *Carousel* - we could not afford to take such a reduction and I had to decline the offer or the idea of a future in pilotage.

Coral Princess - A Murder.

Introduction.

I sailed on board *Coral Princess* between August 26th and November 12th 1993. My relatively short stay proved to be eventful and tragic.

I can remember vividly saying goodbye to little Richard at the airport. My wife Helen had prompted him to say "Bye Bye Daddy" - he did not really understand the reason why of course. It was the first time for me to feel the real pain of leaving the one you've brought into the world when he had started to become a 'real person'. If there had been some way for me to turn around then and support my family in some other way, I would have jumped at the opportunity. My heart and eyes were full, but life goes on - I had to go.

After I had left in 1991, The *Cora Princess* changed to another management company. There had been problems I presume between owner and charterer until she eventually returned to Hong Kong. After many months Sembawang Johnson were again awarded the management contract. A great deal of work had to be done to get the ship back into a seaworthy condition. It was never going to be a luxury liner as it had been let go over the years and the investment required would never be recouped. The ship was put under the Panama flag, reverted to it's previous name and Jan Larson took over command. It was he I was to relieve.

The Operation.

The ship was chartered to Malaysian interests and she began service operating out of Port Klang, the port for Kuala Lumpur, running overnight cruises to nowhere, down to Singapore and the odd trip up to Phuket or Langkawi. The passengers were in the main Malaysian Chinese, some regular cruise or holiday makers plus a large proportion of Chinese Malaysian Junket.

Indications were good at the start of the operation with regular passenger bookings of over 200 every day. Some trips were over subscribed and occasionally passengers had to be turned away. Very soon I realised that the marketing for cruise passengers was separate from the Junket side and it seemed there was very little liaison between the two. On most days there was overbooking in cabins, as many as eight in a four berth. Passengers would come on board and quite naturally would be upset to find they had no bed. There was often a scene at the purser's desk and the charterers representative was of little help.

We had a new Hotel Manager on board, George Lam, who came from Penang and had never been on a ship before. His experience had been on shore with Malaysian hotels on the food and beverage side. Consequently he was very 'green' to shipboard life and Junket operations in particular. Initially he was not helped in the correct way by the charterers representative and was often over-ruled. I made sure that George came to me with his problems when he needed advice, particularly with ship board matters and I would like to believe I gained his confidence, certainly by the time I left he was very open and relaxed, even to the point of being 'laid back' - very unusual, in my experience, for a Chinese.

Problems.

Very soon I wrote a letter to the charterer indicating what I considered could and could not be done with regard to the passenger occupancy. I made it known that even though the ship's stated allowed passenger total on the Passenger Safety Certificate was not exceeded, I considered that to have passengers on board without a berth was effectively breaking the spirit of the law and might be deemed so in a court if there was an enquiry after an accident. My intention was for the charterers to get organised in a professional way, in line with what may be expected within the rest of the cruise industry. In retrospect a far too optimistic hope.

I heard rumours that Eric Yeap, the charterers representative, wanted to have the Captain sacked, along with the Hotel Manager. He was naive enough to mention this in front of the other staff, who quite naturally, came and told me. Pathetic threats from a man who faced a problem by shouting and waving his hands in the air. To have a conversation with Eric was like listening to a long tape which could not be silenced. Two way communication was hardly possible, constructive dialogue was out of the question.

Within a few weeks, a meeting was held in my room during one of our brief calls at Singapore. Our new Managing Director, Kjell Smitterborg, listened to my exchange of conversation with the senior representative from the charterer, Stanley Tham. I reiterated my thoughts on the passenger over berthing problem and Kjell finally stated the maximum passenger number on board would be 438, only some 8 persons below the allowed figure. We discussed and agreed to my handing out a safety memo to those without a berth, instructing them where to go in an emergency, where they should collect their lifejackets, etc. I was told these would only be Junket, who didn't need to sleep and if necessary would 'hot bunk it'.

One has to be flexible sometimes, particularly where your livelihood could be at stake. I backed off a little and said I would monitor the situation. Needless to say it did not improve. The organisation was still lacking and overbooking was done as a matter of course. I wrote a confidential letter to Kjell a few weeks before I left the ship as I considered the reputation of the managers could be at stake in the event of an accident. The response was somewhat overshadowed by other events.

Day to Day.

Staff Captain John Simpson returned to the ship shortly after I joined. We had worked well together before, both on *Cora* and *Orient Sun*. Along with a new Swedish Chief Engineer, Nils Stromberg, we made a good little team, intent on doing the best we could on a ship which really would be more suited as an Indonesian ferry or on a short voyage to a Taiwanese scrap yard. The feeling amongst the crew did not appear to be as happy as when I had been in command before. Uniform was in short supply, hours were long and the schedule arduous. The charterers lack of professionalism and his representative's constant presence tended to wear the staff down, particularly the Pursers and the bar people. Rumour and speculation seemed almost to be a form of entertainment. The Hotel team were affected by a lack of leadership which was a direct result of Eric's interference.

The ship itself seemed to struggle on with a continual flow of defects of one sort or another cropping up. We had no telephones for about three months while we waited for a replacement exchange and all communication within the ship was done by walkie-talkie. Motors kept burning out and had to be landed for rewinding, one of them being the windlass motor. If an occasion has arisen where I would have been forced to drop an anchor, it would not have been possible to pick it up again. Air conditioning always seemed to be on the verge of total failure, to have a cup of coffee would bring me out into a sweat!

We struggled on and the days went by, problems with the charterer and our new catering concession were, to a certain extent, laughed off and our opinion as to their ability was confirmed

MURDER!

Then, on the morning of October 29th, our humdrum routine took a rather unexpected and gruesome turn. John Simpson came into my room at 0730 hours, just as I was waking up with a cup of tea at my desk and said, 'I think we have had a murder!'

This short statement, said quietly and without melodrama brought me quickly to my senses. A feeling of disbelief was probably my initial reaction, murder! - on my ship? John filled me in with the sparse details as we proceeded down to the crew accommodation, I remember seeing crew members standing around as we approached the cabin, all obviously in varying states of shock. On the starboard side of B deck crew accommodation, in cabin PB5, we found the body of Ricardo B Gawat, an engine fitter. He was lying prone on his bunk with his left leg bent. Around the top of his chest and just covering the bottom of his face was a towel, almost completely soaked in blood which had started to go a very dark red, almost black. The head was lying to the left and most of the area around the temple was covered in blood, his black hair was matted where the blood had dried, the man was obviously dead.

I looked around and blood covered the bulkheads either side of his head. It was as though a hose had burst under pressure and just sprayed the area. The dried blood covered the photographs of a girlfriend he had met in Hong Kong, I remembered having seen them on one of my previous cabin inspections.

I was uncertain as to what my reaction would be to see a dead person for the first time, particularly under these circumstances. I had entered the cabin with John not knowing quite what to expect and my heart must have been racing. In a few short seconds I took in the scene. My brain must have searched for an explanation but I did not feel sick or in any way nauseated, even though the situation was most unpleasant. We backed out of the room into the corridor - and I asked myself what should I do? what was I expected to do? Looking back I realise now that I knew there was nothing we could do for the dead man, he had gone and there was no way on earth he could be brought back to life.

The Doctor had been called and was taking his time about getting there. The cabin had to be locked and the body left until we returned to port so that the proper authorities could examine the scene. Doctor Robert came and confirmed death I asked him 'When?' and he thought within the previous two to four hours. The Safety Officer came up with the Polaroid camera and both John and I went back in, I think it must have been then that I saw the wound to the head was not just a gash, but his skull around the temple had caved in. The indentation must have been over an inch deep and as big as a fist. He had been hit by a large and heavy object which had just crushed the skull and obviously caused death instantaneously.

The Doctor had been on *Fantasy World* as Second Radio Officer. He was a Burmese who had taken that professional track as Doctors jobs in Burma were very badly paid. When a vacancy for a Doctor had come up with Sembawang Johnson he was eager and pleased to accept a new contract, although having been away from his country for over a year. I think this incident was perhaps more of a shock to him than for me. He looked grey and very shocked, but as there was nothing more he could do, I sent him away to prepare a statement.

We sealed up the cabin and posted a man outside. The remaining crew who were still milling around in the vicinity I gave instructions to muster in the crew mess. I suppose I was conscious of the effect this news may have on the passengers, as well as the remaining crew who were yet unaware of the situation. My own feelings are that when ever possible, the crew should be told what's happening. I told them, I also asked for assistance or information, but more than anything else I told them to try and keep the news of this incident to themselves and not to gossip. To my surprise, my request must have had some affect, even after we had returned to Port Klang it seemed the passengers were still unaware of the real situation. I had instructed the Hotel Manager to have an announcement made saying we had to return urgently to land a sick crew member.

Investigations.

I returned to my cabin with the Staff Captain to decide the next steps we should make. The safety Officer was told to round up those crew members who lived either side of the dead man's cabin and any one else who was known to have been up late, as well as the Fire Patrol, the crew members who patrol the whole ship twenty four hours a day - they must have seen or heard something.

123

My hand phone could fortunately pick up the shore telephone signal so I dialled the home numbers of the senior company men in Singapore. It was just after eight and they were all on their way to work. I phoned the office and Michelle, one of the personnel ladies had already arrived. I passed on the grim news and asked to get Kjell Smitterberg, our Managing Director to phone me back when he arrived in the office.

The officer of the watch was instructed to make speed for the pilot station at the northern entrance to Port Klang and advise me of our expected arrival time. I knew by then that we must return as soon as possible and try and convince the authorities to take over the investigation, which might be difficult. The dead man was a Filipino, the ship was registered in Panama and was in international waters at the time of the incident. Who was officially recognised as being the authority empowered to conduct an investigation?

I returned to my cabin and ignored the piece of toast my steward habitually brought for my breakfast. Jessy Cabrera, the Safety Officer with whom I had worked with on *Leisure World,* had gathered a few crew outside the bridge ready for me to start interviewing. Looking back it is hard for me to remember to whom I spoke first but gradually a story began to evolve as to a small group of crew who had been left to carry on drinking well after midnight when the crew bar should have officially been closed by the Bosun. Only one of the men, the Fourth Engineer Leo, who was on the 8 - 12 watch, appeared in some way nervous or apprehensive.

I started to come up against a wall, not of silence, but lack of knowledge. The occupants of the cabin on either side of Gawat had heard nothing during the night. The fire patrol saw nothing and I had great difficulty in ascertaining any hard evidence at all. I did discover that the cabin door had been left slightly open, but I did not know for how long. The engine wiper who discovered the body when he went to call him for his morning duty said the door was slightly ajar and the light was off, that was about 0715 hours.

The bridge however had a strange phone call around seven saying that something terrible had happened - this call was later denied. The deck fitter whose bunk pillow was on the other side of the bulkhead from the dead man,

124

a distance of no more than two feet through half an inch of wallboard, didn't remember hearing anything.

I had the distinct impression that the Filipino crew had closed ranks and were going to admit nothing.

The Managing Director called and I passed on the information. He started the ball rolling by informing the authorities, advising the Klang agents of our earlier return, etc.

Arrival.

I continued to interview for several hours until I had to return to the bridge in preparation for our arrival. The berth was occupied by another vessel, but after some discussion the port allocated berth 3 in South Port and we picked up our pilot around eleven a.m. and docked a little after twelve.

The immigration and customs boarded with the agent, but I had to wait around half an hour for the first police officers. They were shown to my cabin and I briefed them as to the situation, also adding that I did not consider that any passenger would have been involved and that I wished that they could be allowed to leave as soon as possible. Their response was at first favourable, but they backed off when they decided they should at first see the body.

I think the sight must have been a little unexpected as they immediately called for assistance from a higher authority. Another twenty minutes or so passed by, more police arrived, checked the body again, and again called for a higher authority. My cabin was beginning to look like a Doctors waiting room with police coming and going, two of the manager's Singapore office team who'd been sent to assist, the company's insurance representative, the charter's representative - all vying for the four chairs in the room.

Eventually a senior police official, a tall gentleman with a turban, arrived on board and along with numerous hangers on, visited the scene of the crime. John Simpson told me that at one stage there must have been ten people trying to squeeze into the single cabin of the dead man! - so much for protecting evidence.

I managed to get a few private words with the official, expressing my concern for the welfare of the passengers, who were still not aware of the real reason for our early return and quite naturally some were getting rather irate.

We had to prepare tables so that as the passengers left they could pass on their names, addresses, etc. Only then did I inform them that a member of the crew had died and that they would be shortly allowed to leave. In the meantime, the body was taken down to the lower ship's side door and landed, without dignity, ashore into the back of a police Land Rover. Many of the crew and passengers looked on as, I'm told, the vehicle drove off with the end of the corpse protruding through the tail gate.

As the passengers were questioned on their way off the ship, a large group of crew were gathered together in a public room ready to be interviewed. The police prepared themselves by having a meal sent into the small conference room. In this part of the world, no food, no work!

Both the charterer and I were concerned for the next sailing. I didn't want to sail with the murderer on board and the charterer didn't want to loose the revenue. He had friends in high places, I did not.

The afternoon ground on with, seemingly, no breakthrough. I tried to keep abreast of the latest news, but there was little. No crew could leave the ship so there was a great deal of sitting around. I think the opinion was that someone would soon be apprehended and we would sail away with everything sorted out - another incident in a busy schedule to forget with the passing of time.

The Inspector built on the information I had given him by interviewing the six crew we knew to have been drinking in the crew bar till 0300 hours. Of course no-one admitted to the crime and suspects seemed thin on the ground. Eventually, after many phone calls, the Inspector said he would take the six ashore for further questioning. He could understand my concern however, and he received permission for six of his men to travel on board for the next trip to Phuket and back. I knew he was under a certain amount of pressure from a higher authority as the charter's had contacts at Government level. He told me in confidence that if he had his way the ship would have been kept alongside for a week if necessary.

The men were taken ashore and the passengers came on board completely unaware of the events of the day. I was told that the police who were to travel would not be down until after midnight - there was some sort of police function on that night, although that was not actually given as the reason for the delay.

Sailing.

We waited till well after 0200 hours and finally sailed just after 0230 hours, even that was an event. The tide was strong and the pilot dismissed the tugs too early. As he went to make the turn, the old ship just carried straight on towards the fishing boats anchored in shallow water. I actually thought the rudder might have been sabotaged by some crew member who didn't want the ship to sail. It could be a relatively easy act to remove the pin which connects the normal steering gear to the emergency system - provided you knew which one to pull, and it was an engineer who had died.

Plenty of astern power solved the problem and as we reached deeper water the ship became more responsive. The system was checked by the Chief Engineer and found to be quite normal. I was tired and my brain had been working overtime. I had to try and think of all the possibilities, all eventualities - no one knew whether the murderer was ashore or aboard.

Even when I left the bridge, around 0500 hours, I could not stop my brain ticking over. I think I even interviewed a few more crew then.

I lay down eventually, still mulling things over. The murdered crew member had not been well liked by everyone. When he had a few drinks inside him he had managed to upset a few people by being hostile. A few weeks before he had pulled a knife and stuck it into the crew bar pool table. The reasoning behind his angerI could not discover, but certainly he had been antagonistic towards three crew who regularly played there, an assistant cook Recto Restituto, Baker Ely Dequina and Chef De Partie Job San Buenaventura. These three seemed to be a clique and were three of the six known to be drinking late the previous night. In fact I ascertained that Restituto and Gawat had been seen staring angrily at each other earlier in the evening.

There was no row or fight however, nor anything else that anyone would admit. The last person we knew to have seen Gawat was Leo Aguilar, the Fourth Engineer who, around 0020 hours, returned the camera Gawat had left in the crew bar. A few other whispers came my way, including one from the 12-4 bridge quartermaster who was in the lavatory outside cabin PB 5 around 0015 hours. He heard Job talking to Gawat outside the door. Gawat sounded intoxicated and Job appeared to be calming him down, but the cabin door soon closed and Job was seen a few minutes later talking to Ely the baker.

This I'm sure was not the time of the murder, however no-one admits to seeing Gawat after this time and it looked as though this was when he went to turn in.

There appeared to be no real motive for the crime. The crew members seemed to have been having a few drinks and playing pool quite happily before midnight, Gawat was even taking photographs of the group. There is something about a closed community like a ship. Relationships look to be fine on the surface, but discontent is often suppressed, feelings are held in check to prevent trouble. Alcohol is often the catalyst which causes emotions to surface and that is why we try to restrict the amount that is available.

I heard another whisper that the reason Job took Gawat back to his cabin could have been to find out exactly which room he was allocated, in preparation for an attack later and there was more than one person involved. I knew Job and Ely from my inspections of the galley and it seemed so unlikely they could have been the perpetrators.

I can vaguely remember seeing flashes of the victims face before I fell asleep even, as is possible on a passenger ship with a large crew. I knew him only slightly as our paths had crossed just once or twice.

The next morning.

I was awake and about before nine. We were going to the island of Phuket in Thailand and due to arrive the following morning. I had my initial reports to write and I wanted to see the senior police inspector, Rahmat Bin Ariffin. Jessy the Safety Officer had already started to assist the police. I discussed with Ariffin his intentions and that I wanted to interview some engineer ratings who were known to have been involved in a fight a few weeks previously, one in which Gawat was also implicated.

During the day, after talking to those involved in the fight, plus their cabin mates, I discovered there had been yet another little conflict of personalities and I believed the wiper, Padernal Resurrection, was no great friend of Gawat. Another crew member Florita Villaver, a motorman, who Gawat went to assist in the engine room fight, also seemed to be someone with something to hide - or perhaps it was just his personality. I was getting confused, there just seemed to be insufficient motive for killing someone.

I passed on my findings to the police and they also interviewed the engine ratings. They started to take finger prints, but I think that was just at my request, as they indicated that they were not expecting them to be of any use. This didn't really surprise me after the way they had all piled into the cabin the previous day.

I began to feel the killing was an accident, that a group of crew had gone into the cabin to teach Gawat a painful lesson, but it had all gone wrong. Perhaps Gawat had struggled and to keep him down one of them had picked up the bar-bell that Gawat used for exercise, brought it down on his head, not realising that the weight plus the energy provided by gravity would inflict such damage. Certainly it had to be a very heavy object, the skull had been crushed by a single blow like a nut between nut-crackers.

The blood had even sprayed onto the carpet in front of the bed, so the perpetrators must have got some on their clothing. Looking back now I realise it would be quite easy to throw bloodied clothing over the side without being seen. The police officers conducted another search of crew cabins. A T shirt was found in Ely's cabin with a spot of blood on and also they found a bloody finger print on his locker. Damning evidence perhaps, but only if the forensic people could connect the two with the deceased.

Another little twist was that we kept finding possible murder weapons - two chipping hammers in the toilet opposite Job and Ely's cabin, a metal paint scraper in the spare drawer in their cabin and another hammer under the washing machines in the laundry room. All these were, I'm sure, planted after the initial search. Obviously someone was trying to implicate Job and Ely, or confuse things even more, or even to get some warped sense of satisfaction by leading the investigation up the wrong path.

All day and into the evening I kept talking to different crew members but was really getting nowhere. I liaised with Rahmat and came to the conclusion they had found nothing significant or he was just not telling me everything. They continued 'grilling' some of the engine crew and both the Chief Engineer and the Staff Captain were not happy about their methods, putting the man in the middle of a circle of police officers and focusing a spotlight down onto his face - sounded to me like something from a spy novel, This was not totally unwarranted I thought bearing in mind the nature of the crime. However we still had a ship to run and our crew were getting both smaller in number and very jittery.

Yet again I went to bed late, tired but still with an active brain. I wanted to be mentally alert the next day should there be a problem with berthing in Phuket. Little did I expect that the events of the next day would give me an adrenaline kick I didn't really need.

Phuket.

The following morning saw us making our approach to the port. Depending on the tidal strength, it can be tricky allowing the correct amount of set as the

130

tide just disappears as the ship enters the channel and the peninsular to the left blocks the tidal stream setting at right angles to the track. We picked up the pilot and officials outside and I made for the entrance.

Maggie, the Chief Purser, came over the walkie-talkie about this time calling for the Safety Officer - another body had been found! The pilot was taking a back seat and I could not afford to loose my concentration. My immediate thought was 'not again'?

By the time we had navigated safely into the sheltered waters of the small harbour Jessy had advised us that a passenger had been found dead in his bed. The Doctor had of course been called and diagnosed a heart attack, not such a rare occurrence on passenger ships which carry a large number of older people. The man had apparently lost $3000 in the casino and was also known to have had a heart complaint.

Needless to say his death did nothing to improve the atmosphere on board. I spoke with the agent and had him arrange for the body to be landed as we had no morgue on board. This also turned out to be unusual as the agent just used his pick up truck to take the body to the local hospital, most undignified.

The Malaysian police had asked me to keep all crew on board, I presume because the murderer, if still on board, might decide to do 'a runner'. In the meantime the charterer decided to take the police off on a conducted tour of the island. They didn't return till just before we sailed, consequently further investigations were not to be continued until later in the evening.

I was curious as to how the investigation was progressing back in Port Klang and I had the ship follow a course which took us closer to Malaysia to enable Rahmat to use his portable telephone to call the police station. He was unable to make connection. Consequently we arrived back in port the following afternoon still unaware of developments.

Return to Port Klang.

After our arrival I was informed that as yet none of those crew already detained had been charged, neither was any other information forthcoming. The police left taking with them Villaver and Resurrection. It was agreed that normal operations could resume with regard to crew shore leave, so in all respects life could return back to normal. There was great disappointment on my part as there appeared to be no progress. Perhaps this was just their way of operating? I knew the rest of the crew would have liked to have seen a result.

We sailed again on another cruise to nowhere and returned the following afternoon. Still no news. The agent said he had tried to visit the men but was not allowed by the police. All we knew was that the police could hold them for up to fourteen days without bringing a charge.

By this time the crew remaining on board were getting restless. Rumours were spreading and I felt it was time I should make a statement. My policy has always been to try and pass on to the crew whatever information that I might have, even if it amounted to very little. I called a meeting in the crew mess for 2230 hours and when I arrived I found the room packed, so full in fact, some were sitting on the floor, jammed by the door and standing in the alleyway. The officers were behind me and I don't think there could have been anyone off duty who was not there.

I asked for silence and the noise dropped to nothing. I could have literally heard a pin drop. They all expected the murderer to be announced I'm sure. I was a little nervous and no doubt repeated myself a few times but I told them the little I knew. I talked for at least fifteen minutes asking them to give me any more information if they had some. I told them that I believed there were some crew amongst them who knew more, to consider their inaction and what it may mean to those held by the police should they be innocent, to think about their religious beliefs and doing the 'right thing'.

I talked of many different things, some of which I can no longer remember, but I finished by saying that, whatever the outcome was, we had a ship to run,

132

passengers to think about and our own lives to lead, 'life is for the living - live!'

I left the room still in silence. I felt emotionally drained - I certainly had never had to speak to an audience like that before. I returned to my room and poured a large vodka and tonic and sat in my big chair to recuperate, Nils the Chief Engineer passed by and said 'that was good', and that was all I needed to settle my own thoughts and make me aware that I hadn't made a complete fool of myself.

Superstition.

The days passed by and still we received no further information. On the sixth day it was brought to my attention that the purser's girls were sharing the same room at night, scared. Maggie talked to me and explained how frightened and superstitious they were. There had been a crew raffle a few evenings before. I had gone down to lend a hand with the draw and to try and spread some goodwill. I pulled out the three winning numbers. The third prize number was the number of Gawat's cabin. The second prize number was the cabin number of the deceased passenger. The first prize was won by the ticket which had been allocated to Gawat but he had failed to pay his money so it had been resold to Danny the barman who was one of those ashore at the police station. All this was, of course, a coincidence, but with the Chinese belief in the unnatural, it didn't really go a long way to calming the nerves of our crew.

I had permission from the police to clean out Gawat's cabin. His remaining belongings had to be collected and itemised ready for landing before being returned to his wife. The complete utility gang went to clean the cabin together, moral support I guess. Whatever furnishings remained I instructed to be taken to the garbage room, including the blood soaked mattress, carpet and curtains. Photographs of the girlfriend were disposed of and all other items were cleaned to make sure no blood remained on them. The cabin was scrubbed out more than once and then repainted till there was no trace of the violent act which had happened within. I didn't really expect anyone to want to use the cabin, but in fact less than two weeks later it had been allocated by the Hotel Manager to a new Burmese fitter, who was obviously unaware as to why his cabin was so clean. He was pleased no doubt to have a cabin on his own. I wasn't told whether his attitude changed after he finally heard the story.

The following night was the seventh after the murder and for the Chinese this is very significant, the more superstitious believe that on this day the spirit of someone who has died violently will return. The charterer arranged for a medium to come and clear the cabin of any evil spirit. They were more worried I think for the effect on their casino business than our crew!

My own suggestion was that the Junket would think that the ship was unlucky and that therefore they, the players, would be lucky on the tables, thus there was a likelihood the passenger carry would increase.

Maggie and her girls were still frightened. I let them be together for one more night but I spoke to her the following day. They had to brave their superstition. As officers they should set an example to the other crew and if they couldn't, then they should put their resignations on my desk. A little hard perhaps, but it worked.

Friday and Sunday saw the ship back in Singapore, I discussed with the office my thoughts as to who I believed should leave the ship if the murderers were not charged. I believed that after such an event it would be better to 'clear the decks' where possible. Until most of the crew who had been on board at the time had finally left the ship, there would always be talk, rumour and bad feeling.

The outcome.

On Monday morning, on our way back to Port Klang, I received a telex advising me that the eight crew members had been released from police custody and that they would be coming down on board later in the day to pick up their belongings before being repatriated to the Philippines the next day. I was shocked and amazed.

After discussing the news with the Staff Captain and the Hotel Manager I decided to refuse to let them on board. I thought that once the crew realised that they had been released then perhaps there might be some retribution. I was quite sure that the crew really believed that Job and his friends were the culprits. I also didn't want them on board talking about their interrogation. Stories get embellished and many things which really should not be talked about could come out.

We docked. The agent arranged for their belongings to be taken to their hotel and I tried to get information from the police station. Rahmat came to the phone but said he had been on leave and had just returned that day. He would try and let me know on the following Wednesday what had transpired.

One of the Hotel Officers, a friend of Leo Aguilar, heard the news and went to the hotel to return some jewellery which he had looked after. When I spoke to him later he told me that Leo believed the killer to be still on board, Job and Restituto had been beaten every day but had not confessed. All of them were apparently looking forlorn and hungry. Prison had been no holiday, which I'd anticipated, but I had seen no alternative, the murderer should be discovered.

Conclusion.

Looking back it is hard to believe that the police could not have found the culprits. All possible suspects were on board, they could not leave, the evidence was there for all to see, surely with today's modern crime solving techniques it should have been a relatively simple matter. We were not originally impressed with the performance of the police, but I am not a policeman. The original cabin searched had been cursory, their questioning seemed to have been without direction - all the crew that were taken ashore were the names that I had given the police.

I waited for further information from the police, none came. I now consider that perhaps, because the ship was not Malaysian, was not in Malaysian waters at the time of the murder and because the victim was not Malaysian, the case was quietly dropped. They had insufficient evidence and no confession. I also consider that the police were under pressure from a higher authority, contacts in the Government which the charterers had in their palm. A greasy and wealthy palm which lubricated the wheels of authority to ensure their business continued unhindered by the bad publicity which would surely be generated by a conviction.

I had just five days to go before I was to be relieved by Captain Larson. All I could do was complete the paper work and pack my bags.

There is a sad conclusion to the story. After the eight men were sent back to Manila and allowed to escape from any possible justice, the wife of Gawat sent a telex to Sembawang Johnson asking the company to do all they could to ensure the perpetrators of the crime be caught and punished, as some small justice for her and her four children. She believed the company to be honourable and the Malaysian criminal system to be fair. She believed in the righteousness of God. I think she would soon believe in man's inhumanity to man and without the income of her husband she will have to rely on the generosity of her relatives to support her family through the long years ahead. In a country where poverty is a way of life and the chance to rise above the masses is just a tenuous thread, hers had been broken.

Empress Katerina

Checking my discharge book I found I was assigned to the steamship *Empress Katerina* from 23rd February to 23rd March 1994, just a month, the last week of which was spent in a hotel in Singapore. Kjell Smitterberg had 'invited' me out to join the ship in the yard prior to it re-entering service for a Malaysian charterer whom I had previously met. He expected I would have to 'get my hands dirty' - and that turned out to be an understatement. The ship was an unmitigated disaster!

The vessel had originally been built in about 1951 as the *Patricia* for Swedish Lloyd and their service between Sweden and London. There is no doubt that when she entered service she must have been a lovely and delightful ship to sail on. Much of the original panelling and decorations within the ship were still in situ, including a stone fireplace which would have seemed more suited to some baronial hall. Of course the decor was looking more than just a little 'tired'. The ship was of some 6,542 Gross Tonnes and had classic lines, although the shape of the funnel had been changed many years previously to give a more modern image.

There had been several owners and many names over the years. She had spent many years with the Greek Chandris Line who had finally sold her about five years previously to a Greek Cypriot. It would appear that he had started a short cruise operation between Cyprus and the Near East but this had obviously not been a remarkable success as she later made her way to Vietnam to 'star' in a film called 'The Lover'. The ship had been there for quite sometime before the owner sailed her over to anchor in Singapore roads which is where the charterer, Irene Ng, had first seen her.

Arrival.

The day I turned up, the ship had just been put into the Jurong dry-dock and the view from the dockside was not encouraging. Years of neglect were evident and the growth of weed on the underwater hull looked like something from a reef formation. In fact we measured some of the fan coral which was over a foot in length, the grass even longer and the thousands of barnacles seemed to be cemented in place.

I boarded in the early afternoon after having a direct flight out from London followed by a briefing in the office and lunch with Kjell. There were between twenty and thirty Semjom staff now living on board plus a further twenty or so of the owners staff, a mixed bunch of Poles and Burmese, with an Egyptian cook thrown in. The accommodation was, to say the least dismal, old, dirty and small. I was given a passenger suite room - sounds good, but with no air conditioning and no hot water (not that you needed it with the ambient temperature) it was no palace.

I saw a few familiar faces and met our Staff Captain, Martin Johnson. He had been in town for over two months, going out to the ship whilst it was at the anchorage, making out defect lists, stores required lists, etc., etc. He showed me around and told me his tales of doom and gloom, all not very encouraging but I had an open mind and was determined to give it a chance. I was soon to be disillusioned by the attitude of the owner, who apparently was living in a top hotel in town and coming down to the ship to monitor the refit. According to the Charter Party, the owner was responsible for getting the ship back into Class while the charterer had agreed to get the Passenger Ship Safety Certificate. I learned that the owner had no money and could only pay for repairs, etc., by drawing down on the Escrow account which the Charterer had set up with the bank. She had even paid off the creditors who had had the ship arrested because of unpaid bills.

The representative from the P & I Club, Swedish Club, was on board to ascertain whether it was in their clubs interests to insure the vessel. A meeting in the ships dining room, which became our general office and meeting place, ended up with a certain amount of acrimony between the various parties. The surveyor wanted to see all records pertaining to the vessel and the report from GL (Germanishcer Lloyd Classification Society), however the owner, Nicholas Patias, was reluctant to release anything. The Charterer, Irene Ng, arrived and tried to smooth over the waters and even suggested to me that there was a special way to deal with this man to avoid hurting his pride - I thought we'd come to get a ship back into service!

Inspections.

From the brief inspection I made the first day I realised that there were major defects, with large steel repairs to be made in the trim tanks. These looked like they had been 'doubled' by ships crew using plastic steel instead of weld metal. In other words repairs had been made which were purely cosmetic to get the ship through survey and hope a conscientious surveyor was not asked to check.

On my second day the underwater hull area was inspected, scraping of the whole area was taking place und was to take two days. Intake and water chests grids were removed and the propeller scraped. Two blades were found to have serious cracks which would necessitate repair, the rudder pintle clearances were taken and one was found to be zero. By this time the owners technical representative was starting to get more than just a little agitated, not only with the owners 'secretive attitude' but also with the fact that the yard had still been given no order to carry out steel work repairs. In the meantime, grit blasting of the hull commenced in the late afternoon.

The third day, when priming was started on the hull, resulted in me finding more than just one or two defects outside, loose rivets, deep pits in the steel and a cracked weld by a void space. I made notes and passed them onto the yard. Steel repairs were finally ordered by the owner for the tanks,

Our men started making up other defect lists within the ship, crew cabins - which were a mess, galley, lifeboats, bridge, radio room, etc. Much needed to be repaired or replaced. More of our own hotel crew were arriving on board to start the clean up and begin painting out their accommodation.

I found several holes through the hull shell plating over the next few days, from the engine room and also the butchers shop. We checked the anchor cable and found many studs were loose and needed welding. On the following Sunday (27th.) the propeller was finally taken ashore for repair. The hull painting was coming on well - this was probably due to the fact that the charterer was paying for it! Outside a vast improvement could be seen but inside great problems were being experienced in the way of the steel repairs to the tanks. 'Grey', water was leaking onto the tanktops which prevented welding taking place. The owner was blaming the charterer for putting to many crew on board and thus overloading the sanitary tanks, this in fact was not strictly true. The flushing water had been switched off, but toilets, etc., were being flushed using buckets and as the large sewage tanks filled it became more and more apparent that they were rotten and leaking like a sieve.

We kept our own spirits up, mainly by cleaning up in the evening and drinking 'one or three *Tiger* beers' - our favourite brew of Singapore. The ship was so hot inside that all day the boiler suits worn just stuck to our skin. To take a shower was only momentary respite because the sweat came back before drying off had been completed. Sleeping was only possible by laying out without clothes or a sheet - I was one of the fortunate few who had a fan! The food was good, our own chefs did a great job in the grotty galley and came up with some pretty good results.

By Wednesday 2nd. March, the underwater painting had been completed except for repairs to holes, trim tank repairs were continuing slowly and superintendent Maw arrived. Irene had insisted Sembawang Johnson should appoint a technical representative to monitor the progress. On the Friday the owner employed a new superintendent when the first had thrown his hand in, obviously totally discouraged. We continued to find evidence of much steel wastage in other areas, around the stern frame, above the double bottoms 1 and 2, in the void spaces behind the reefer boxes. The underwater area steel had been repaired and the propeller refitted. The owner was asked to confirm the stability for the vessel when it lifted off the blocks. We knew he couldn't and we knew the stability was below the required criteria because his crew had been playing around with the tanks to accommodate the cleaning of fuel tanks near the void spaces, which had to be emptied and cleaned to allow burning and welding to take place.

Undocking.

On Saturday 5th the dry dock was flooded and we were towed out. There had been some serious discussions before hand and I refused to take any responsibility for the stability. In the end the list was only 5o to port - enough to get a few people worried. A leak was discovered in the hull down in the machinery shaft tunnel where an oil covered cement box was found and water was coming in at about the rate of a normal tap flow. The interesting thing was that this cement box was within a few feet of where the GL surveyor must have stood to examine the water pressure test on the repair to one of the shell holes. No action was taken, but the Jurong yard insisted the ship had to leave the yard. They were fed up with the attitude of the owner and his prevaricating when it came to work orders, etc.

The ship was towed about five miles to the Atlantis ship yard, where we tied up to a large pontoon in the late afternoon. Kjell and Irene arrived and we tried to impress on them the severity of the defects we had found and the lack of progress with the owners repairs. Our crew had been living in poor conditions for a week and I decided to try and get some of the auxiliary plant operational, even though it really wasn't our responsibility I felt we had to move forward otherwise we would never meet the Charterer's intended schedule. We had to find out everything that didn't work and it was no use relying on the owners word that everything was fine and dandy! I knew it would take more than just the few days he promised to get all the ship services operational.

141

The flood.

On Sunday 6th I asked our own Indian Chief Engineer, Prem Singh, to see if he could get the sanitary water on line. By the afternoon he'd managed to get about 50% of the system operating at a relatively low pressure. All seemed to be coming together fine, with a gradual reintroduction of ship services, however, my initial misgivings were soon to be justified.

I think it was about 1930 hours and we were sitting around chatting about the lack of progress on the owners side with steel work repairs, drinking yet another *Tiger,* when the Chief had a sort of panicky call over his walkie-talkie from our Junior Engineer standing watch in the machinery spaces. I decided to accompany Prem down below, where, as we got closer, we could hear the intermittent but rapid sounds of water falling around the forward area.

On closer examination we found that the port sanitary tank drain line had collapsed. The pump used to empty the tank to the sea was cutting in and out when the float switch was being operated, first by the sanitary pump filling the tank and second as the level dropped when the tank contents deposited themselves onto the double bottom tank top below. The ship was basically trying to sink itself from the inside! I ordered the sanitary pump stopped while we took stock of the situation.

Prem, Martin and I started climbing around behind the port auxiliary boiler, into the void space around the sewage tank. Here the water was rushing down and disappearing through an unwelded seam in the steel plates which were part of the repair to the stabilising flume tanks. As the port tank filled it would have eventually flooded over to the starboard side if left unchecked.

Meanwhile on the starboard side I discovered something even more alarming. The starboard sewage tank was leaking out in the surrounding void space also and here it could be seen that the fluid level had reached a certain level above the double bottom tank top before the sewage pump had cut in and started pumping out both the tank and the void space. The ship started to take a starboard list and the void space fluid disappeared to the ship side as

142

the water found it's natural level. Then I noticed water bubbling up through the tank top, the top of the double bottom tank below the void space.

What this effectively meant was that all the tanks and spaces in this area of the ship were connected by holes or corroded steel. There was no way of isolating a particular double bottom tank, void space or even sewage tank. In my estimate, assuming this was indicative of the steel condition throughout the vessel, hundreds of tons of new steel would need to be brought in, thousands of man hours would be involved and surely the cost would be astronomical. This could only mean further delays to the date set for cruising and quite possibly an abandonment of all initial plans.

In the meantime we were back to buckets and the engine room tank tops were covered with a large quantity of oily brown water. The later was obviously of no particular importance to the owner's engineer as he promptly pumped the whole lot into the dock, leaving a large slick to slowly disappear into the darkness with the tide!

Fire.

The next day saw a meeting between owner, charterer and manager. The owner promised to provide a schedule as to when we could expect the ship's services to be reinstated, but little work was being carried out on his side and the general frustration level was high.

On Tuesday 8th. March we had our fire. The yard, who had been reluctant to start further work until the owner had given some money on account, had just a few men working in the void space behind the main fridges. Access to the space was limited and burning tools had to be passed through a large lightening hole behind a passenger cabin bulkhead. The void space itself was about thirty feet long six feet high but only two feet wide. Many of the steel web frames were corroded and bent in way of the ship's side. These needed cutting out and replacing.

A worker had been using burning and welding equipment in the space. Looking back now it would appear that he put the tool down when he went off for his afternoon break and did not switch off the electric current. Consequently, the electrode, which was lying near some water, caused the wood and cork insulation of the fridge, exposed by the corroded steel, to catch alight.

By the time we were alerted the smoke was getting quite thick in the area. I instructed our crew to get everyone not required to leave the ship and to get out what Breathing Apparatus we had. Martin took one set and went for the fridge entrance. I took another and made for the lightening hole to the void space.

As fires go it was not yet serious, but access to the seat of the fire was difficult. Fortunately the smoke was not too bad outside in the cabin where I was preparing to enter the void space with a hose. Crew members were assisting and trying to couple up the hose, nozzle, water supply, etc, while I donned the BA set. I soon discovered I could not get through the hole with the BA on my back, so I slipped it off, indicated for the guys to hold it while I climbed through. They thought the set was to be removed and proceeded to try and drag it away, but of course the mask was still attached to my face by the air tube and I was breathing from the set. For a few moments there were scenes reminiscent of a comic opera while I gesticulated furiously from inside the space to pass the set back through so I could put it back on. The mask virtually denies you from having a conversation with anyone more than two feet away and when these are Chinese or Filipino all you get in return is looks of complete incomprehension!

The hose was passed through and the water was switched on. This had to come all the way from the shore, so there was no instant reaction to my command of switching it back off again when I found the connection of nozzle to hose was not tight, thus depositing more water on my shoes than in the general direction of the fire which I could see smouldering about six feet away. In the end some normality came back to the situation. The visible fire was extinguished and I backed out from the void space.

I had managed to just about communicate with Martin via our walkie-talkies'. He had seen the fire from the inside of one freezer room, flooded it with water and come out closing the door behind. We discussed the situation and I decided to see what he'd been up to, so we donned our BA's and re-entered the room. I felt around the stainless steel cladding behind which was cork insulation. There were still hot spots and these seemed to be getting larger so we ripped some of the cladding from it's supports and tried to feed the hose behind. We had a modicum of success as the smoke certainly seemed to die down.

By this time the yard had galvanised themselves into action and all sorts of people started to turn up. We had a discussion with their fire people who then proceeded to dismantle the cladding and rip out the cork insulation and the wooden joists supporting. One or two of these had burnt through and the fire had been progressively working it's way along inside the insulation.

I went down onto the floating pontoon where the crew and Irene were waiting, happily chatting without any apparent concern. She asked me why I was so wet when she thought it was supposed to be a fire?!

Martin and I both talked about it afterwards and realised that none of the owners crew had bothered to assist in any way. In fact the owner, who had been on board , was seen to have gone off ashore sometime during the episode and he didn't return till a day or so later. We both wondered why we had actually bothered, it wasn't even our ship! In fact the only thanks we got were from the shipyard who realised without our intervention the fire could have become very serious and, not only would it have cost them a considerable amount of money, but they could have had a burnt out wreck on their doorstep to contend with.

Out to anchor.

There was still no further work given to the yard the next day by the owner and it was quite obvious to me that they were most frustrated. The owner already owed a considerable amount. We saw his superintendent come on board with one or two people and we began to realise his intentions. He believed the yard were charging too much and intended to take the ship to the anchorage and have the work completed by subcontractors.

I considered it was unsafe for all our crew to be on a ship at anchor which had inadequate lifesaving equipment. None of the lifeboats had been down in the water for possibly years, there was no way we could ensure a fire could be put out using the ships pumps and fire main, and even the emergency generator was out of commission because of a cracked cylinder head. I informed Semabawang Johnson of my concerns. I was told to try and test the boats.

On Saturday 12th, we finally managed to get number 1 lifeboat on the starboard side into the water. The davit arms had stuck through lack of use and maintenance, but we greased, pushed and generally cajoled the boat down. There were a few minor leaks which we remedied and I believe we even got the engine to run - our engineers had been trying to overhaul them as best they could. However we found holes had corroded through the steel davit arms close to the support for one of the rollers. This would definitely result in new davit arms to be fabricated if a surveyor saw the corrosion and the boat would not be available for use till repairs had been completed.

I was in a way despondent because of the degree of neglect, but also quite cheerful because I thought now surely our management could not expect us to live on board?

In the early evening Kjell came on board with Kanawati, another chap from the office. When he walked into the dining room the ship had about a four degree port list. As we sat down to talk the ship just rolled slowly through about eight degrees and settled with a starboard list. This was nothing new to us, we had been complaining about the lack of stability for days and I knew, for the time at least, it was not too serious. Kanawati, however, looked like he was about to wet himself - "It's, it's still going!" he said, as Kjell looked on - and I slowly smiled.

I think only then Kjell realised that what we had been saying all along was true and not a gross exaggeration. I took him up to show him the davit, he looked at the rest of the mess and said he would phone Irene.

146

This, I think, was really the beginning of the end of this ship for us. Kjell came back and said that many of our crew would be flying back to the Philippines as soon as possible and the remainder would stay with the ship for the moment. I was to try and check the situation with the remaining boats.

On Sunday morning forty of our crew disembarked and the ship was towed out of the yard to the West Jurong anchorage where we arrived around ten thirty. The owners crew still remained, along with a few shore cleaners to prepare the area around the trim tanks for welding. The government chemist sent to check for gas free had not passed the space fit to burn and weld. The remainder of the Semjom crew left the ship by 1730 Hours. I left four on board to keep a security watch and to monitor what the owners crew were doing while the rest of us were taken to The Great Eastern Hotel in town. Initially it was Kjell's intention to return during daylight hours and continue with our work but to have the security and comfort of a shore hotel at night.

The last week.

From that time on we spent every night at the hotel, commuting by coach and boat every day, a tedious journey which took almost one and a half hours in each direction.

Subcontractors for the owner came out and proceeded to do yet more cleaning around the void spaces and removing asbestos insulation in the machinery spaces. This was to access the area for burning, but I noticed virtually no protection was being used to ensure the very dangerous asbestos dust was contained, even though I advised the chargehand. The subcontractors finally left the ship on the Tuesday after the chemist still refused to grant a gas free certificate.

In the meantime we attempted to get number 2 lifeboat into the water for testing. Many precautions were taken to prevent a mishap, but when we tried to lower the boat the friction brake just collapsed, corroded away around the break lining. The boat proceeded to drop at an increasing speed and I had visions of loosing the bloody thing altogether. The davit winch, none of which had worked when we first came on board, was applied as the boat fell.

Unfortunately the winch motor had been re-wired the wrong way round, so instead of trying to lift the boat, it tried to increase the speed of it's downward momentum. The extra lashings held, just. The winch wiring was quickly corrected, the switch activated and the boat started to climb slowly back to the stowed position.

The lashings had started to part by this time but as it reached the top, the harbour pins were rammed home into the davits and the boat came back to rest, safe in the stowed position with the davit arms run back so that the harbour pins took the weight.

I instructed all brakes to be removed and their condition checked. The davit arms were also in the process of being checked and of course we found more evidence of local corrosion. After another couple of days, by swapping brakes bands, we felt confident to try number 2 boat again. This time the electric motor control box caught fire and we were back to square one!

By the Wednesday I had to instructed the engineers to check everything they could get into, even though the owner had instructed that we were not to touch anything without his permission. We already knew that the turbine had debris inside the casing, but we had not looked inside the boilers. This turned out to be an interesting exercise, the fire brick linings had been incorrectly repaired and inside the starboard boiler you could actually look through the bottom into the bilge. If they had tried to fire it up, it would surely have set the engine room ablaze! The boiler water feed tank was contaminated and slowly leaking, the general condition around the outside of both the main and auxiliary boilers was one of total neglect and corrosion.

It was surely now just a matter of time. Eventually on Saturday evening I was advised by Kjell to start removing all the equipment the charterer had put on board. We began the next morning and by 1630 hours three barges had been loaded with everything from mattresses to ropes and washing machines. A great effort by all our remaining staff.

The decision had been made by the board of the charterer to leave the dispute in the hands of the lawyers. We left the ship that evening not to return, leaving only a fire watch on board and that was only till Monday morning when the initial insurance paid by the charterer expired. The remaining crew were repatriated over the next few days and I flew back to England on the Wednesday evening, financially not so well off, but having gained a lot of valuable experience as to what can go wrong in these type of situations.

Less than a month later I joined another ship in Port Said, *Santiago De Cuba,* which was to be renamed *The Empress,* hastily chartered by Irene to fill the gap left by the *Empress Katerina.* Many of the original crew returned and needless to say they were more than happy to be on a ship that was in service. The accommodation was at least habitable and the services worked.

There is a small humorous incident which I will always remember. The ship, being owned by a Greek Cypriot, was registered in Limassol, Cyprus. After the hull had been cleaned and painted a lovely dark blue, the name and port of registry on the stern was picked up in white. Towards the end of our period in the Atlantis yard we were getting increasingly frustrated with the stalling and downright lies of the owner and something inside me wanted revenge, of a sort, so I instructed Martin to get the Bosun to paint out the LIM from LIMASSOL. Kjell was not over impressed, but still took a photograph.

We changed it back a day or so later and I'm not sure whether Nicholas ever saw it - but I am quite sure he must have heard about it by now!

The Empress - Collision.

I flew to Cairo and journeyed onwards the next morning to Port Said along with three other senior officers to join *Santiago De Cuba,* a ship which I had previously seen in the colours of SeaEscape as *Scandinavian Song.* Built in 1966, the ship had had a chequered history with her longest period of stable ownership being during the seventies when, as *Saudi Moon 1* she had operated as a pilgrim ship between Egypt and Jeddah - not exactly romantic.

And so it was that we took a hot and bumpy drive in a well battered Peugeot down the excuse for a main road towards the entrance of the Suez canal. The last thirty odd miles were in almost nil visibility as we became engulfed in a sand storm, the intensity of which the locals had not seen for many years. The dusty streets of the town were reminiscent of some wild west film and when we arrived in Port Said, the muck had even worked it's way up to the third floor of the agents office.

Brief formalities were followed by another car ride to what can best be described as a modest Egyptian 'retreat' - a beach hotel obviously designed for the indigenous population and with none of the glamour of the Caribbean equivalent. The reception area was filled with people all clamouring for a room, the dust and dirt filling the air and covering the furniture giving one the impression of a construction site on a busy day. Somehow we managed to be given three rooms and we passed the rest of the afternoon waiting for news. Our ship had missed that nights convoy through the canal and we had to stay till the early hours of the next day. We had a meal, tried the local beer and even some Egyptian wine - the first, and after the experience, definitely the last time.

The agent's man came for us around six the next morning and another bumpy drive was followed by a thirty minute run out in an ageing work boat to meet the ship as she entered the canal - not stopping, but slowing down just enough to embark us and the rest of the inevitable Egyptian entourage that always seems to board for these canal passages. I was to meet again Glan Phillips, the Master I had relieved on the *Scandinavian Saga*. He was bringing the ship over with crew from the owners, International Shipping Partners. Irene Ng, the Malaysian lady who had intended to charter the *Empress Katerina,* had found the vessel when her previous efforts to start a cruise operation had flopped. She had the marketing arm of Empress Cruise Lines all set up in Kuala Lumpur and had to have a ship. *Santiago De Cuba* had just been laid up after an aborted attempt to cruise out of Cuba, so she was chartered to fill the role with the intended name *The Empress.*

We left Port said on April 23rd 1994 and sailed on towards Singapore with a call at Aden for bunkers and a slow down off Sri Lanka to pick up a few of the new crew. The ship was old and well abused. We found many deficiencies during the delivery run, many poor repairs which competent staff would never have made - and the crew accommodation was filthy.

In Singapore we had just a few days before we were to sail again for Port Klang in Malaysia, the intended home port. There was little time to get the crew on board, yet alone complete the safety drill to the surveyors satisfaction, I had to cajole the crew by threatening hours of drills into the night if they didn't reach a proper level of competency. They responded well and we left on time and there followed many months of trading. We gradually improved the vessel, had our problems small and large, but generally the ship maintained the schedule of one day cruises out of Port Klang and Penang with the odd call to Singapore.

I completed my contract and left in late August for a six week break, the Staff Captain Martin Johnson taking over. I returned in early October for what was to be a voyage to remember. A collision must be a Master's worst nightmare, when the speed of events make rational decisions difficult and the outcome is one which is truly in God's hands.

I had fired one of the Filipino bridge watch officers for incompetence, his ability being at times rather frightening. In his place a Burmese arrived, Mr. Kyaw Sein, a tall man in his mid thirties with the gentle manners of that class of people who have been, for too long, subservient to all they believe to be their betters.

I allowed him time to settle into his new position. He had come from a car carrier and had no passenger ship experience, but he was in his own way keen to work, tidying out the wheelhouse and even labelling all the bridge cupboards. What he lacked became evident quickly, the qualities of leadership. I pointed out the necessity to take charge of the crew when necessary, make them work the way he wanted - the way I wanted.

I learned from the personnel manager that he had had a bad report from his previous Captain for poor cargo work performance, not a good sign when I knew that on a passenger ship I needed someone who could work and think independently should a serious problem occur during the night when I would be asleep or in the event of some disaster such as a fire.

On the evening of November 28th., we left Singapore close to schedule on a cruise to nowhere with the intention of returning the following afternoon. The weather was fine, the visibility was clear and we took the direct route out to sea via the western pilot boarding ground, the pilot disembarking shortly before 2300 hours.

I handed over to the 8 - 12 watchkeeper, Mr. Lazarte, one of the more competent Filipino officers I've had the pleasure to work with. I went down below and prepared my night orders which were to advise the watchkeepers to stay on one engine and proceed to the north west until such times as it would be necessary to cross and return down the south east traffic lane of the Malacca Strait for our return journey. These I returned to the bridge, had a brief check at the traffic situation and then went off to my cabin.

I must have been dreaming. All of a sudden there was a tremendous jolt, enough to almost shake me from my bed. For a split second I thought I'd had a nightmare but the ship was still moving unnaturally, I thought, "My God, he's hit a fishing boat!"

There have been occasions before when I've had to get on the bridge quickly, so I have my clothes all ready to jump into, even so, my fingers fumbled with my trouser zip and shirt buttons. I raced out of my cabin almost falling over the contents of my fridge, tins of coke and beer having thrown themselves out and laying in my path. I barged past the Chief Purser and someone else in the corridor reaching the bridge in something under forty five seconds - so I was later told.

The Second Officer was close to hysterical, screaming at me that there was no one on the bridge of the ship with which we had just collided, I could see our lights reflecting dimly from the superstructure of a vessel close on our starboard side and went out onto the bridge wing. My heart was already in my mouth but what I saw frightened me even more.

The port side of the tanker was against our starboard side, both ships appearing to be proceeding in tandem onwards into the darkness. I have heard of tankers exploding after a collision, consuming all the oxygen in the vicinity and causing all on board the two ships to be asphyxiated before a huge fireball totally destroyed the vessels within hours. In my own mind I knew that we had to get away from the other ship before it exploded. I knew that the tearing of steel could cause that little spark which would be enough to ignite any oil gasses that were of the right inflammable mixture.

I raced back into the wheelhouse to find the port engine still going ahead and to see the rudder was hard a port. I blew the whistle in attempt to attract the attention of the crew of the tanker, who may not even have felt the bump. The bridge of their ship was over three hundred feet behind us, the bow the same distance ahead. Below our bridge wing were the tanker's cargo manifolds. I had no idea as to the size of the ship except that it was considerably larger than us.

Back on the bridge wing as I looked over the side, our bow started to gently come away as we gradually turned to port. Our belting rubbed against the tanker as she appeared to move ahead and finally the two sterns separated. My first fears were, for the moment, gone. Now I had to consider whether the collision had caused structural damage below the waterline. I closed the watertight doors because if more than one water tight compartment was breached the ship would surely sink.

By this time all the deck officers were on the bridge. I gave instructions for the tanks to be sounded to check for ingress of water. The Norwegian Staff Captain, Geir Larsen, made a public address telling everyone not to panic - a fine gesture, but his clarity of English was not so good and I knew broadcasts which people could not understand in this type of situation may cause further confusion so I made another. I had to take a check on myself, to make sure my voice appeared calm, talking firmly but quietly and advising everyone that there had been a collision, that we were checking for the extent of damage and that they should remain calm at their muster stations until I made a further announcement.

The number of thoughts that must have gone through my brain during the next minutes and hours were numerous, too numerous to remember, except perhaps the one that suggested that this event could lead to my future at sea being curtailed, particularly if I didn't do what may be expected of a competent Master after an accident such as this.

Very soon I had reports that there did not appear to be any water coming in. The ship was still upright, had not taken a permanent list and therefore progressive flooding was not likely to be a problem - unless something gave way. I knew that the lives I had under my trust were, for the time at least, safe. A great relief.

The forward stores were checked and the lights on the foredeck were switched on. It was then that the structural damage became patently obvious. The starboard bow bulwark was completely distorted over a length of about thirty feet, in some places having been bent down to the horizontal. Inside the Bosuns store there were three large and jagged holes, fortunately all well above the water line. We had been struck by the tanker a glancing blow in possibly the safest place, the flair of the bow. Another ten or twenty meters astern and she would have surely run over us, penetrating the ships side and into the water tight compartments - we would have sunk in minutes.

The tanker was loaded with 120,000 tonnes of crude oil. The ship therefore was considerably larger than our meagre 9,000 tonnes. One fortunate aspect was that the tanker was fully laden. A tanker in ballast is far more dangerous as the empty fuel tanks, unless inerted, have an oil gas inside which, when mixed with air, can easily become explosive and a mere spark would have caused the terrible explosion I feared.

I dispatched the Staff Captain to survey the damage. The safety Officer was walking around the ship reassuring passengers and the Chief Engineer was in the engine room having stopped the main engine after we had phoned down to get the duty engineer to respond to the engine room telegraph. My accident report describes in brief detail a catalogue of errors made by the bridge and engine watchkeepers. The actual true sequence of events will never be known but I was later to make continued investigations to get at the facts.

Within ten minutes of the collision the South Korean Captain of the tanker came on the VHF radio and we briefly exchanged ship's names, etc. I was too busy to have a long discussion in his disjointed English but I asked him to stand by in case we were in need of assistance. Later the Staff Captain spoke at greater length with the ship to exchange further details. After our situation had become clearer I phoned my Managing Director and gave him the news. He took it well and assured me he would contact the authorities, Charterer and all those who needed to be made aware of the situation. My hand phone had already been ringing several times, but I had decided not to answer as I knew it would be our Charterer who had probably been advised by her representative on board. The last thing I needed was a distraught woman asking me questions I could not, as yet, answer. As it was, a few hours later when I spoke with her, she asked me whether the ship could not just go straight back into service, the damage being repaired on route!

From my investigations, the sequence of events started probably an hour or more before the collision. The overtaking tanker, *Ocean Success,* had been detected by Kyaw Sein on the radar sometime before 0130 hours. He realised the vessel was overtaking and that if it kept on the same course the closest point of approach would be five cables, or half a nautical mile - not a great deal but acceptable in the narrow and busy waters of the Malacca Straits.

Some time after 0200 hours he detected on the radar a vessel travelling in a reciprocal direction and ascertained that this would pass close down the port side.

From my questioning, the Second Officer admitted that about 0220 he realised that the tanker, which was now almost on the starboard beam, had altered course to port by some ten or twenty degrees. The computerised radar gave a new indication that the closest point of approach was zero and that would be in just over twelve minutes. The south bound ship had a closest point of approach of less than two cables at around the same time. He therefore realised he was in what we call 'the sandwich' and his only real course of action at that time should have been to slow down - he did not. Instead he tried to call the tanker on the radio but received no reply. He flashed the Aldis signalling lamp at the tankers bridge, but still no response.

By this time he must have been getting panicky. He was on his own on the bridge as he had allowed the lookout to go and assist the fire patrolman in cleaning the swimming pool. The lookout had a walkie-talkie, but he wasn't called till after the collision. A few minutes before 0230 he realised he should slow down. By now the tanker must have been looking very large on the starboard side. He rang the engine telegraphs but there was no response from the engine control room.

Down below, the Filipino 4th. Engineer left the engine room around 0235. He said later that he had stomach problems and needed to use a toilet, so he had gone all the way to his cabin. The Junior Engineer, even though told to stay in the control room, left to check around the main engine in use at the time. The oiler was also out, seeing to the boiler, consequently there was no-one to answer the Second Officer's telegraph command. Kyaw Sein said he

156

also tried to phone the engine room, this would have sounded an alarm in the engine spaces, neither the Junior nor the oiler heard anything. I can only assume the Second Officer possibly rang the wrong number in his haste - or that he lied.

For some inexplicable reason Kyaw Sein put a position on the chart at 0230 from the satellite navigator, just three minutes before the collision. When asked why he answered me by saying that he thought the position of the collision would be important in any ensuing enquiry. In other words he had by that time accepted the fact that a collision was inevitable. Later on that morning when checking the chart, I found that there had been some erasing of the original pencil marks and Kyaw Sein admitted that he'd done some 'correcting' as the original was not clear enough. In fact he had rubbed out the fixes not once but possibly three times. This was evident because I had instructed the chart to be photocopied a few hours after the event and some positions remaining on the chart did not coincide with the photocopy, some were actually missing and others did not correspond with the speed of the ship.

Regrettably Kyaw Sein forgot to call me. The standing instructions advise that the Officer on Watch should call the Master if in any doubt or if concerned in any way. It is possible that I might have been able to do nothing to avert a collision occurring, but assuming he had called me soon enough I believe I could have turned to port just before the collision and cut in behind the south bound ship.

The other 'mystery' ship appears to have passed close down the port side at about the same time as the collision, 0237 hours. Kyaw Sein believed it to have been about one cable away, but there seemed to be some doubt as to it's existence as he was the only one to have seen it. I would have thought that any ship coming in the opposite direction, seeing both visually and on radar, that a collision situation was developing close to his track, would have altered course away from that point - unless of course it was yet another ship keeping a non existent lookout.

A great many people moved very quickly after the impact, including the 4th Engineer from his toilet. The casino was busy and the passengers inside were escorted to the upper deck muster station by the staff. These Chinese casino staff were one of our weak links regarding safety and I had only the day before ensured that they knew exactly where to go in an emergency as we had anticipated a drill in front of surveyors when we were in Singapore that day - if the collision had been a week before they may have been less aware of their responsibilities.

The engineers finally responded to my request to stop the engine after Lazarte telephoned them in the control room which had become manned again after they had felt the bump. Eventually some semblance of order came from the chaos and I was able to feel confident that we were not going to sink, that I could take the ship back to Singapore and that our lives were not in danger. It seemed like hours, but within twenty minutes I had made a second announcement to the passengers and crew advising them all to return to bed.

We could not immediately get under way because the Second Officer, in his last few seconds before the collision, had gone over to hand steering from automatic pilot, and somehow managed to get his wrist stuck in the spokes of the small wheel when the jolt of the collision had knocked him off his feet. A pin inside the auto pilot had sheared and it took us a few hours to fashion a new one. Once that was fitted we slowly increased speed and headed back. I wanted to take it easy initially in case any of the water tight bulkheads had been weakened. By that time the tanker had also got under way and was making for Port Dickson in Malaysia to discharge her full cargo. Fortunately she received only minor damage and there had been no oil spilt from any of her tanks.

I retreated to my cabin to prepare my initial report to the managers. I had to retype it as my lap top printer took this moment to expire, no doubt having suffered from the severe jolt and instant travel across the desk at the time of impact. By the time it had been faxed off we were heading into the congested waters of the Philip Channel off Singapore. I stayed on the bridge until after arrival and then waited for the onslaught of authorities which I new were bound to descend into my cabin. The true scale of the damage only became apparent as we looked from the dock and from one of our lifeboats used to take photographs from sea level. It was impressive enough but not the disaster it could have been. We had several local shipyards come down to climb all around and prepare quotes for the repair. The time the ship would be out of service was also a factor to be considered as the cruises were booked up well in advance.

That day was to be first of many I would suffer being questioned by the Singapore authorities and the insurance surveyors. The Singapore Straits Times had us on the front page the next day and fortunately I was praised by one passenger for giving 'calm announcements' although he also commented there should have been lifejackets in the cabin - not in fact required on this ship as they were all on deck at the muster stations.

Two days later we sailed round to the Sembawang Maritime Shipyard where the repairs were to take about ten days. It was a busy time but we managed to complete other work as well. I believe my position was vindicated but the Second Officer and the two engineers were removed from the ship prior to sailing. Lessons were learned and we closed a few loopholes in the system. The managers finally realised that a better quality of officer was required even if it meant paying a little more. Experienced men with good references would in future be employed

For me, the morning after was a beautiful day. I looked out of my window at the bright new day and felt that it was really good to be alive. To survive such an accident with no fatalities or injuries was luck indeed, but also to come out of it with my reputation intact was perhaps even a bigger miracle.

I never heard what the outcome of the P & I Club investigations were as I was to leave the ship in early January and join another vessel in March with another management company. Consequently I have no idea whether the true story was the one the Second Officer gave, or if the officer on the tanker was never actually on the bridge. One unusual aspect of the case was that the tanker was fully loaded and therefore with a deep draught, too deep to have safely navigated over the underwater banks which we had easily crossed with our relatively shallow draught of six meters. Perhaps the navigator of the tanker had realised too late his situation and had set the new course on the auto pilot taking him towards deeper water and not considered we could be in the way. Even so, it is very difficult not to see a passenger ship on a clear night when the lights are visible for ten miles or more.

Before Kyaw Sein left the ship he came to my cabin. He insisted on paying his respects to me. I was his father on the ship he said, went onto his knees, bowed three times and then shook my hand. I was both embarrassed and touched. He was being dismissed from a job he no doubt badly needed, but in a way it shows the culture of these people who accept fate far more readily than those of us from the west. He had arrived with no ships in his almost new discharge book and I was not allowed to add comment when he left, so he left with no ship's stamp. It made no difference, there is a always a ship owner willing to employ sailors with a license provided they are cheap enough. Two weeks later he came to see me again and told me he was joining another ship the next day. Another Master would have an officer who could give no evidence of his previous employment - or his reasons for leaving.

RUMINATIONS FROM A MASTER.

– Or how to drive an ageing twin screw, twin rudder passenger ship with a bow thruster but no bridge control.

Introduction.

Even though I had worked on passenger ships for over ten years, the day I took over as Master was probably one of the most nerve racking in my life. I had spent three weeks with the previous Captain, doing the 'driving' on some days and occasionally making a real hash of it! When the incumbent says 'OK, I'll take over now' and promptly proceeds to stop both engines and put them full astern it does tend to dent your confidence just a little. I would often end up kicking myself and asking why the hell the beast wasn't doing what it was supposed to do? - The engines were screwing the right way, the rudders were in the right direction, the thruster was pushing the right way!, Why?!

It is quite simple really, ships do not always behave in the way you expect. In fact they rarely appear to do the things you were taught as sea school. Every docking with these ships is different in some way or another. Every ship is different, the ground rules are there - but the rules are not cast in stone. The aspiring passenger ship Master, quite obviously, has to spend much time watching his mentors, questioning what they do and why.

There will be Masters who will pick up the skill quickly, there will be others who will take many hundreds of dockings before they feel confident and there will be others who will always feel more confident if the pilot docks the ship. For all there will be dockings which, now and again, will cause at least minor palpitations! The scary docking is a great way of finding out your not quite as good as you believed yourself to be.

In the past four years since I became Master, I have been in command of five mainly ageing passenger ships. I have completed countless dockings and undockings, frightened myself a few times, been close to a breakdown watching Staff Captains learning not to approach the dock at over five knots - and always wondered how I could give to other potential drivers what I was not given myself.

So here's a few words from 'the old man'!

Rule number 1 - and probably all you need to know.

Always appreciate that ships don't just go forwards and backwards, they go:- forwards, backwards, sideways to port, sideways to starboard, the bow can go to port and to starboard, the stern can go to port and to starboard - and when the bow goes to port it doesn't mean to say the stern is going to starboard - and visa-versa. It can crab to the left, crab to the right and any thing else in between.

In other words, just about the only direction the ship will not go is up or down. (under normal circumstances). You have to feel it, wear it, sense it - just don't try to understand it.

Rule Number 2. Small speeds, small dents. - but sometimes this doesn't work either, speed is manoeuvrability.

Rule Number 3. Always have 'one bell' left in reserve - old American expression for not putting the telegraphs against the stops - in normal situations.

Down to Basics 1.   Undocking.

Taking off is always easier than landing - that's why I'm starting this way round!

I always teach the aspiring Staff Captain how to undock first, sounds logical of course, but there is quite a lot to learn here which will make life simpler and less terrifying later. What is important is to try and treat the ship as though it was floating in air, then attempt to move it bodily in the direction you wish to go, against the forces which are acting in other directions.

When you wish to come away from the dock, the tidy way is to move bodily sideways away from the quay. This is very pretty, but not always practical, depending on the power of your thruster or the transverse moving power of your propellers and rudders acting together. To get the back end off, go astern on the inboard engine and ahead on the outboard engine, at the same time thrust off at the bow - easy? - don't believe it.

If you do this on an engine control ship you will almost certainly discover that you cannot guarantee both engines to start simultaneously and that you'll either go marching up the dock towards the ship in front, or worse, the other way towards the ship behind. This is not so desirable because the Second Mate on the stern will start to panic and give you totally erroneous distances to the impending collision (Another rule - put little faith in the distances given to you, or at least until they get below five meters)

This method of leaving the dock is very fine for learning the balancing act with the vessel, but the best way is to thrust the bow in towards the dock first, (if your ship has a bulbous bow don't be to eager) then go astern on the inboard engine and make sure you have revs before putting the outboard engine ahead. In this way, if the outboard engine does not start, then at least you won't hit anything! If, by some misfortune, the engine does not fire then stop the other. Assuming you have two rudders (it's a pain if you haven't) and you find the stern is going out too quickly, put the rudder hard over in the direction which will bring the stern towards the dock, at the same time as you are thrusting the bow away from the dock.

The Master has to watch and remember where he has put the telegraph handles, watch the tachometers, watch the bow and stern, and watch a transit to the side - you have to be aware as soon as the vessel starts to move forward or astern and counteract, sometimes very quickly, for what is not going right. The more experienced Master will not rush into something which he knows will need split-second thinking to counteract problems which may arise. Therefore he will avoid trying to do a sideways manoeuvre if, for example, he only has ten meters clearance either end. (normally no problem at all with controllable pitch)

Always attempt to think of your next move, what problem is likely to occur and what you need to do to correct it. Then be prepared for the unexpected. Move well away from the dock before you try to turn the vessel, be aware of the current and wind. Check what may be anchored in the vicinity or what's heading your way, turning through 180 degrees can often take a lot longer than you expect.

When the wind is blowing strong onto the dock you may find that you can get the bow out with the thruster or the stern out with the engines, but not both at the same time. Passenger ships usually come up into the wind when going astern. Thrust the bow in as much as you can then go half astern on both engines. The ship will back off the quay and turn into wind at the same time, but be careful - you may have to thrust the bow off to prevent it coming into contact with the dock as you start to turn. Providing you have good stern power this should not happen, but this is a bold manoeuvre not for the faint hearted. If you start to set down onto the dock go 'full astern'. Also beware of the ship astern, as the bow turns towards the quay it is also turning and possibly setting down towards whatever was behind you!

Another useful manoeuvre when you need to turn through 180 degrees after leaving the berth is to turn short round right at the dock. Not quite so dramatic as it sounds. First thrust the bow in and the stern out, thirty degrees or more if possible. (you can hold onto the forward spring for a while if your worried about creeping forward). When all lines are clear, full thrust the bow out, it will come out usually faster than the stern will come in. Put the wheel hard over to lift the stern off the quay then go ahead on your inboard engine. I

164

know you're now thinking the stern will come in towards the dock by going ahead on the inboard engine, but in practise the twin rudders will keep the ship off. If the stern still creeps in, ease back on the bow thrust. If the stern comes off too fast then ease the rudder. Once the stern has come off far enough you can back on the outboard engine if necessary. This is a very satisfying manoeuvre which can keep the stern within six feet of the dock as you turn - any closer than that is perhaps being a little to adventurous! Probably wise to advise the pilot as they tend to get a little nervous with this one.

If the current is coming fast from the stern and you have to turn 180 degrees then a similar move is handy, but bringing the bow close to the quay. The current is usually stronger away from the quay, hence this manoeuvre. If you do not have a bulbous bow then this makes life easier, but it is surprising how deceptively close the quay looks from the bridge. Trust the distances you get from the Mate (under five meters!) and make sure you can always go at least 'one more bell' astern on the inboard engine.

One way of ascertaining whether the ship is moving ahead or astern is to eyeball the thruster wash. This should be going straight out if your turning within your own length.

If the wind is blowing off the dock (God's tug) you could try just letting all the ropes go at the same time. However, it is inevitable that one end will come off quicker than the other. I find it is best to single up then let the head lines go first, waiting then to see if the bow will blow off. Providing the stern doesn't rub up against anything nasty this can be very handy. All that has to be done next is to let go aft, make sure all the rope tails are out of the water and power away. If the wind is very strong normal precautions should be taken to prevent the final ropes parting before being let go. The thruster can, of course, always be used to give that extra push to get the bow out into the stream.

Down to basics 2.   Docking.

Now this is where things can start getting tricky. I think the most important thing to remember is that if your approach is bad then your docking will prove to be difficult or even impossible without using a tug. Any angle between about 40 and 60 degrees to the quay is usually OK. Anything less can lead to some more palpitations if the ship starts to set bodily towards either the berth or the ship you have to pass to get there.

If you have to turn through 180 degrees to stem the current (always best) leave yourself at least two or three ship lengths to sort yourself out after the turn is complete before you get to the berth. If the tide is strong you will probably drift that distance if you start the turn as you pass the berth. Do not start the turn with too much headway. With twin rudders I usually stop the engine on the inside of the turn, that way, if the ship doesn't turn fast enough you can then go astern on that engine. If you have too much speed that engine might prove difficult to put into the astern mode - the engineers may have to brake the prop by wasting air first. Air is a commodity not to waste on these type of ships.

On the majority of occasions once I have started the turn and put the inside engine astern (what will be the outside engine at the berth) I do not have to stop it until the lines are all out and the vessel is secure. Similarly, if no turn is required, once I am committed to the approach there is no need to go 'through the gate' with either engine. The inside engine should be turning ahead and the outside engine turning astern to bring the stern onto the dock. The speed in either direction can then be adjusted with the corresponding engine and the twin rudders to control the sideways direction of the stern. The thruster is used to bring and hold the bow on.

Now, here's what we need to look out for:-

Wind. Look at the flags. Passenger ships are affected considerably by the wind, particularly at slow speeds.

Current. Look at the ships at anchor, or better still, the cooling water coming from ships near the berth. You can always ask the pilot of course, but you will be surprised how often they get it wrong.

Both wind and current must be used to your advantage, in just the same way you use engines, rudders and bow thruster. If you try to ignore them you will come a cropper.

When you first take over command do not try to drive the ship straight onto the berth. You must work as though you are trying to park it away from the berth by about one and a half ship widths. Once you get to this point move the ship in bodily sideways (this skill you have learnt during your undockings) Don't expect to make an approach parallel to the berth initially as it tends to be rather slow with most ships. Work the engines and rudder to bring the stern in and the bow with the thruster, as all ships have different characteristics it is just part of the learning curve to decide which end to bring in first. If in doubt, try getting the bow in so a spring can be sent ashore, then work the stern in by holding on the spring, but do not put too much ahead power on the inboard engine as the spring may break causing much consternation on the foredeck. Then even more with you as the ship starts to charge up the dock.

After a while you will be able to judge relatively easily how much power to use and which way to attack this situation.

Assuming no wind or current (it happens!) then after a few dockings the aspiring ship handler will be more positive with the approach. Make sure the angle is right but be aware of how much space will be left either end after alongside. If you take the bow in too early the stern will come dangerously close to the ship you have to pass to get into your berth. If the sun is on the offshore side, look for the shadow your ship makes at the stern and this will give you an indication of how far you need to come ahead to clear.

Remember, with a bow thruster, you can usually get the bow in, therefore leave the bow out and the stern even further out until your quite sure the stern will clear as you come ahead into position. This leaves you with one less worry, particularly if you find the wind or current is doing something you didn't expect.

As you get close to the dock, have the heaving lines sent ashore (you should not need to use a line boat) and make sure the crew only send ashore one and one first and take in only the slack. If they put weight on, it will spoil your balance with the ship and one end or another will come into the dock. Your intention should be to hold the ship a few feet off the dock until the lines are well out of the water, then let the ship settle against the fenders and hold her there with the thruster and the engines. You will probably have to adjust the rudders to balance the push of the thruster. Do not let the men send any more lines till one and one are fast as they will only get confused, ropes will end up in the water and may get caught up with the machinery spinning round beneath. I would be very surprised if you had enough men to handle more than two ropes each end at one time anyway.

If there is a current and you have to turn through 180 degrees, remember that your ship will be moving bodily sideways, even after the turn appears to be completed, so give yourself plenty of room. I have scared myself a few times when I realised I was sliding towards the ship behind my berth. The bow thruster is not very effective when you have more than three knots forward speed. So don't expect it to get you out of trouble. Use more astern power on the inboard engine. If in doubt stop the outboard engine and then go astern on that as well. Once your forward momentum has been taken off the bow thruster will then be effective.

If the wind is onshore be wary of settling onto the dock too quickly. Again you should aim to parallel the dock about fifty to a hundred feet off and feel which way she wants to go. You may have to change the engine configuration with the inboard engine going astern and the outboard going ahead to keep the back end off. In fact I have found that because the stern tends to 'suck up' into the wind, I often have a job to get it to settle onto the jetty in these conditions.

When current and wind are onto the jetty, the ship handling Master can have his most 'interesting' time and much concentration and quick reaction may be required not to make a hash of the whole thing. If the wind is off the dock then much power may be required first to get the ship into the berth and secondly to keep it there while the men are making fast. The Master will, by experience, know when the wind is getting too strong to berth without tug assistance. I have found it's usually something over twenty knots, but this of course will vary from ship to ship and the direction from which the wind comes.

With wind against current it's anyone's guess which one will predominate, however more often than not, depending on the strength, it will be the current.

One other point, if you come in too slow, both wind and current will affect you more. Therefore there will be occasions when a faster approach will be necessary to counteract the outside forces, and if you realise too late that you are too slow, a bump may be inevitable. If you are not sure before hand, keep your distance or take a tug.

Finally, when you have one and one fast do not be distracted by, for example, muttering sighs of relief to the pilot. The job is not over till you've rung 'Finished With Engines' - all sorts of nasty things can happen before all the lines are secure!

Conclusion.

My ruminations are just a few pointers in learning to drive this type of ship. There are many, many more situations where these guide lines won't be of assistance, but the only way the ship Master can become competent at ship handling is to have constant practise, in all conditions. If you work on single screw freighters, or on vessels where the pilot always takes over and instantly makes fast two tugs then ditch this into the out tray!

To all you experienced Masters who would totally disagree with what I've written then all I can say is that this is what's happened to me. I know the type of ship I command is in the minority, however they do exist and by becoming experienced at handling them we can save the owners or charterers money by not having to take tugs. That doesn't mean to say we will not take a tug when the need arises, it means we ascertain by experience the limits and capabilities of ourselves and the vessels that are put under our responsibility.

I 'drive' my ship in and out of port every day and ship handling is one aspect I enjoy. At first I wondered how long my heart would work under the nervous anticipation of the next docking, now I look forward to each 'stand by' knowing I have attained a skill few of us have the opportunity to practise.

To those of you who aspire to 'driving' your own ship, remember, every time you take over the controls it is part of your learning curve and any docking where you have no paperwork to complete afterwards may be considered as a hundred percent success.

Captain Philip Rentell. MNI.   **November 1994.**

Published in the Nautical Institute magazine "Seaways"